FORTY FAKE AND PHONEY LETTERS

TORN CURTAIN PUBLISHING
Auckland, New Zealand
www.torncurtainpublishing.com

ISBN Softcover 978-1-991299-31-4
ISBN EPub 978-1-991299-32-1

All scripture quotations in this publication are from the New International Version®, NIV®. Copyright © 1973, 1978, 1984, 2011 by Biblica, Inc.™ Used by permission of Zondervan. All rights reserved worldwide. Many verses have emphasis added by the author.

Typeset in Minion Pro, Oswald and Poppins

Cataloguing in Publishing Data
Title: Forty Fake and Phoney Letters
Author: Stuart Watt
Subjects: Religious humor, Biblical interpretation and hermeneutics, Bible characters, Historical fiction, Christian faith and understanding, Christian gifts and resources.

A copy of this title is held at the National Library of New Zealand.

FORTY FAKE AND PHONEY LETTERS

Laugh your way through the Old and New Testaments with this recently-discovered haul of unverifiable (but surprisingly insightful) letters.

Stuart Watt

CONTENTS

Introduction   1

A Note on the Dates   3

Letters Relating to the Old Testament of the Bible   5

Adam and His Rib   6

Noah Builds a Boat   11

Moses and His Red Sea Problem   16

The Wonderful Wall of Jericho City   21

Delilah to the Rope Company   26

An Almost Defeated Army   30

850 Dead Prophets   34

A Naughty King and 102 Dead Soldiers   40

Three Young Men and a Very Hot Fire   44

The Old Man and the Lions   48

The Prophet and the Whale   54

Letters Relating to the New Testament of the Bible   59

Zechariah Almost Burns His Finger   60

Unexpected Pregnancy, Secret Divorce   65

Still Pregnant but No Divorce   70

The Christmas Story   73

Who Did You Say We Are Related To?   77

A Little Whine Brings a Lot of Wine   85

Peter Nets a New Job   89

Business Advice For Jesus   94

The Sad Story of the Hard-Done-By Finance Men   98

Tricky Questions for Jesus   104
Peter's Insurance Claim   109
More Insurance Problems for Peter   114
Jesus and the Jerusalem Medical Council   118
Money Changers   124
Career Advice for Jesus   128
We Are Taking You Off Our Client List   134
Judas Seeks Legal Advice   139
Return of the Fisherman   144
I Say, Is That a Tear in the Curtain?   149
A CAT and DOG (and Mr T)   155
Peter's Reputation Rehabilitation   161
A Jurisprudence Nightmare   167
Things Turn Deadly in Real Estate   172
The Man They Couldn't Kill   177
Bodyguards for Hire   185
And Then There Were Four . . . Gospels   190
Treating Women the Wrong Way   197
Prison Problems   203
The Biggest Change Since Sliced Bread   208
Stay Connected   214
Acknowledgements   215

INTRODUCTION

These forty fictional letters take a humorous, tongue-in-cheek look at various events and people depicted in the Old and New Testaments of the Bible. Since I have taken a little 'artistic licence' in my dramatisation of certain scenarios, I encourage you to read the original biblical accounts on which the letters are based. This will reduce the likelihood of anyone believing that Joseph and Mary actually did have an argument over her new sandals (they didn't!). More importantly, without a robust understanding of the Scriptures, it is far easier to be led into error by someone misquoting a verse or sharing a story out of context.

Each letter is followed by a discussion section focusing on relevant topics, questions, and beliefs. These are intended to function as a quick summary rather than an in-depth study— as each topic could easily fill an entire book in and of itself. It is my hope, however, that the discussion material will provide enough information to assist those who want to dig deeper. Many Christians read very little of the Old Testament, yet it contains some of the best-known stories in all of Scripture. Furthermore, a Christian should spend time in the Bible because, as the apostle Paul wrote, its contents were written for our benefit (Romans 15:4).

In general, the most current source material (especially in more technical fields) is found on the internet, yet website addresses often change or sites shut down. Where suitable, I have chosen sites belonging to larger organisations in the hope they will continue operating for a longer period. Even books and magazines can become difficult to source. Many books eventually go permanently out of print, and libraries tend to keep back issues of magazines for only a few years. Still, the information that has been provided here will hopefully be a sufficient starting point for readers wishing to investigate matters of personal interest, like how a Jewish woman ended up owning a piece of the WWII Auschwitz extermination camp.

How to look up a scripture reference in a Bible:

Reference Given	This means to look up and read . . .
John 3:16	Book of John, chapter three, verse number sixteen.
Romans 10:9-10	Book of Romans, chapter ten, verses nine to ten.
James 4	Book of James, the entirety of chapter four.
Luke 6:43, 45	Book of Luke, chapter six, verses forty-three and forty-five (skip those in between).
Hebrews 9:15, 27-28	Book of Hebrews, chapter nine, verse number fifteen as well as verses twenty-seven though twenty-eight.
1 John 1:9	Book of 1 John (or 1st John), chapter one, verse number nine.

A NOTE ON THE DATES

The further back one travels into history, the more difficult it can be to accurately date an event. Different dating and calendar systems, incomplete or non-existent written records and records containing no dates at all can pose a significant challenge. Consequently, the dates assigned to these letters may not depict when the events in question occurred with complete accuracy. I have sometimes based dates that appear in the letters or the discussion sections on estimates from those familiar with the particular topic under discussion. That said, even scholars working in the same field can arrive at dates that differ by years or even decades. For example, dates spanning decades have been suggested for when each New Testament Gospel was written.

Over the centuries, many different calendars have been in use (and still are) including Jewish, Chinese, Julian, Egyptian, and Babylonian. As time passed, some had days and even months added to improve their accuracy, creating some confusion. For example, in the modern Georgian calendar that most of the world uses (certainly for synchronising international events and transactions), December is the twelfth month despite having the *Dec* prefix meaning 'ten'. Originally, the Roman calendar started in March and finished in December—the tenth month. As more months were added, however, December eventually became the twelfth month.

With respect to Jesus, most estimates put his birth at around 4 B.C. to 6 B.C. (per today's Georgian calendar) where B.C. represents "Before Christ" and A.D. stands for *Anno Domini*—Latin for "in the year of our Lord." This B.C./A.D. system (no zero year recognised) wasn't in use until around 500 years after the death of Jesus. Many secular writers prefer to use B.C.E. and C.E.—Before Common Era and Common Era—as these are viewed as religiously neutral terms. Therefore, 500 B.C. would equate to 500 B.C.E.

LETTERS RELATING TO THE OLD TESTAMENT OF THE BIBLE

ADAM AND HIS RIB

Genesis Orthopaedic Clinic

Eden Medical Centre

Havilah

Adam

First Man Enterprises

East of Eden

Date: 1st Millenium

Dear Adam,

I'm writing to update you on the results of the x-ray we took during your last visit. On that occasion, you mentioned God had previously put you to sleep and when you awoke you discovered you were minus a rib but had gained a wife. I bet that was a big surprise! Tell me, before the rib's removal, had you been experiencing a nagging pain in your side? Just wondering . . .

The story goes, that before your wedding there was just you and Eve, and the wedding location was an absolute paradise—well, until that mix up involving *someone* (I'm not naming names) eating the wrong piece of fruit. Haven't you heard, one should always read the terms and conditions that go with any product involving an apple.[1]

The good news is, your x-ray is completely normal—dare I say, even perfect. However, I've been thinking about that business of being put to sleep and having your rib removed to make a wife, and it got me wondering . . . if it was done once, maybe it can be done again? I've since assigned two graduate assistants, Anna and Thesia, to look into it. Anyway, you have twelve pairs of ribs—twenty-four individual ones—which is exactly what I expected to find.

---

1   Although popular culture has Eve eating an apple, the fruit in the Bible is unnamed.

There's no need to bring your children in for x-rays. You see, Adam, it's the same as if you were to cut off the tip of your finger. Any child you had after that wouldn't be born missing the top of their finger. In the same way, if you lose a rib, or even five, that doesn't mean your children will be born with fewer ribs. I've lost count of how many men I've had in my office convinced they are missing a rib and requesting an x-ray to check. You may not be aware of this but, unlike all the other bones in the human body, rib bones can actually regrow.[2] As your x-ray shows a full set of ribs, I imagine it probably grew back already, or God replaced it. Now, I'm not one to listen to rumours, but did Eve really say she was hoping to marry the perfect man but would settle for one who was missing a rib?

I must say, there are men in my fishing club who are somewhat envious of you. When I asked them why, they said you were the only person they knew who not only has no mother-in-law, but that she never even existed. How sorry you must be to have no-one to send you last-minute notes saying they're coming to stay for the holidays or to ask questions about when you and Eve are going to have more children.

One advantage in your kids not having grandparents is it won't take them long to draw their family tree. That said, a family tree that short is sure to invite a fair bit of scepticism, and I can imagine there would be those wanting to show your family on one branch and a chimpanzee or bonobo on another.

Yours,

Amos
Consultant Orthopaedic Surgeon

---

2 www.elifesciences.org/digests/40715/ribs-hold-the-key-to-better-bone-healing

DISCUSSION

THE EXISTENCE OF GOD

Most English translations of the Bible mention God by the fourth word, "In the beginning, *God . . .*" (Genesis 1:1). The Bible begins by explaining what God did, and that includes creating life and the universe. As God has eternally existed (Psalm 90:2), he is outside of the physical universe and time. Even so, creation acts as a witness to humanity of God's existence, though some choose to reject it.

> *For since the creation of the world God's invisible qualities—his eternal power and divine nature—have been clearly seen, being understood from what has been made, so that people are without excuse.*
> *Romans 1:20*

THE ORIGIN OF HUMANITY

Genesis states that when God created humanity, he did so in the form of male humans (the first being Adam) and female humans (the first being Eve). Both were created in God's image (Genesis 1:27). As both men and women derive from the same human genetic material, they are equally human from a biological perspective[3], neither having superior humanity.

THE FIRST MARRIAGE

Jesus stated the first two humans were joined together by God (Matthew 19:6), producing the first marriage and creating the first family (Genesis 2:24; Matthew 19:5). This is the only occasion in all of Scripture when God bonds two people together in a 'one flesh' relationship, and he does so in a sinless environment (the Garden of Eden). As humans, Adam and Eve are given a joint directive involving reproduction and the taming of creation.

> *". . . be fruitful and increase in number; fill the earth and subdue it. Rule over the fish in the sea and the birds in the sky and over every living creature that moves on the ground."*
> *Genesis 1:28*

RULERS VS. OWNERS

Adam and Eve were made rulers over creation, *not* owners. God, having created the earth, claims ultimate ownership (Psalm 24:1). Humans are mere caretakers, and in many ways, we are currently doing a rather poor job.

---

3   Men and women share the same DNA material but differ in their X and Y chromosomes. Also, a woman, when pregnant, can grow a placenta whereas a biological male cannot.

THE ORIGIN OF HUMANITY

Over the years, people have formed the impression that Christianity is not compatible with science. Some even go so far as to claim that Christianity is anti-science. This is misleading. Both believers and non-believers have made major contributions across the disciplines; non-believers certainly aren't the only ones achieving results in science. There can be a difference in opinion, however, when we discuss the topic of human origin—in other words, where theology meets biology.

How did life begin? Secular scientists currently don't know and can't replicate the process. Even if we accept that evolution explains how life-form A becomes life-form B, it still doesn't explain the origin of life itself. If we accept that a rock is not alive but a cat *is* alive, then where did the 'alive' inside the cat come from?

Not only is there much that science can't yet explain but its toolkit is not always well suited to answering certain questions. For example, why, as a life-form, does humanity expend effort on art, music and mathematics when none of them are needed for our fundamental survival? Science has generally focused on the 'how' of human origin but struggles with the 'why'. Why are we here? Is life, and humanity in particular, just the by-product of an accumulation of random, unguided, physical, biological and chemical processes, or do our investigations point towards the involvement of a divine being?

Many would argue that the Christian view of origin—that is, life being the work of a loving creator God—is a better explanation for the incredible complexity and interconnectedness that we see. Such people would also argue that God originally created the world perfect, but the flow-on effects of Adam and Eve's sin has resulted in death, decay, sickness and struggle. This perspective provides a better basis for understanding and explaining such things as morality, good and evil, consciousness, and the pursuit of non-essential endeavours.

GOOD AND EVIL

The Bible links the creation of Adam with two things:

1. The beginning of humanity (Acts 17:26).
2. The arrival of sin into the world (Romans 5:12).

If we claim Adam and Eve never existed as distinct individuals undescended from a previous life-form, then the question of the origin of sin remains unanswered. If humanity arrived by random evolution, two uncomfortable implications emerge.

Firstly, humans are nothing special with respect to life-forms and are just another step along the primate evolutionary pathway. Secondly, without God, there is no fixed morality. Right and wrong become value judgements we make both individually as humans and collectively as a society, and they are subject to change—'right' today can be 'wrong' tomorrow, and vice versa.

Without a fixed point of reference (God's moral code), nothing can be said to be absolutely wrong. 'Evil' becomes just another aspect of evolution at work, and people like Idi Amin of Uganda and François Duvalier of Haiti are nothing more than unhelpful collections of atoms. With atheistic evolution, moral accountability stops at death, so if you never get caught for committing a crime, you never have to answer for it. Following this reasoning, Nazis who arranged the deaths of millions of Jews in gas chambers during World War II and were never caught before dying, simply got away with it.

There is much the Book of Genesis doesn't tell us when it comes to human origins, but it does tell us there is a creator God and there *is* moral accountability, even after death. It is our choice to believe if there is more to life than what we can see and touch, or whether the here and now is all there is. Of course, just believing the here and now is all there is, doesn't actually make it so.

NOAH BUILDS A BOAT

Maritime Safety Authority
Nautical House
Mount Ararat Vistas

Noah
Shipwrights & Co.
The Plains of Ararat

Date: Before the Rain Fell

Dear Noah,

Several weeks back, one of my senior inspectors visited you on site to discuss your ark-building project. You will be pleased to know the name HMS ALL ANIMALS AFLOAT remains available in the shipping register. One thing I do need to ask, however, is why you are building the thing so far from any water?

Regarding moving the ark, you said, "Don't have any plans, don't need any; God will supply water directly to the site using rain." It was a novel answer for sure. So novel, in fact, that the maritime meteorology office say they've never heard of rain and they await the event with much interest to see the stuff for themselves. They are hopeful there'll be enough to collect to take back and analyse. A quick calculation suggests forty days' worth of this so-called rain will be needed to float the ark. Call me a sceptic, but that's an awful lot of something that no one's ever seen.[4] I do seriously suggest you seek an alternative moving solution.

In the absence of rain, and allowing for the vessel's significant weight and size,[5] an

---

4 Genesis 2:5-6 suggests prior to this event, moisture was delivered by mist and streams—it had never yet rained. The floodwater was a combination of rain and the 'fountains of the deep' (Genesis 7:11)— subterranean water gushing up through large cracks in the earth's crust.

5 The ark was 300 cubits (approx.140 to 150 m) long and 50 cubits (23 to 25 m) wide (Genesis 6:15).

official plan to move the ark to open water will be required. It will be important to ensure that the move doesn't occur on any festival day, as traffic levels are already chaotic enough. The number four on-ramp for the Garden of Eden Expressway is the one closest to you. However, it is currently closed and is expected to remain so for some time after that unfortunate incident involving the stampeding elephants colliding with the stampeding rhinoceroses. In my view, the sooner the Giant Nephilim Highway gets built the better—that and upgrading to the new International Babel signage system.

On a side note, our night school offers the Boat Skipper VLV (Very Large Vessel) qualification if you're interested. One of our greatest concerns is your lack of maps, flares, and any form of ship-to-shore communication. Your response to the question about emergency flares was, "There won't be anyone left around to see them, let alone launch a rescue mission." Not an entirely professional attitude, but that aside, there is also the matter of the ark lacking any form of propulsion. As things stand, you risk being blown off course and—dread the thought—even running aground on a mountain. The only way to guarantee your safety would be if God himself was looking after the ark, and how likely is that? Frankly, you put far too much confidence in God—certainly far more than the Maritime Safety Authority feels is justified. Religious people can drown just as easily and quickly as anyone else, you know.

You stated the cargo will consist mostly of animals, food, and a crew of eight family members. I've been asked by the SPCA (Seafaring Passage of Caged Animals) inspector to check if you have obtained an export licence for the Giant Pandas, and if you are also familiar with equine quarantine procedures? In addition, if you intend to breed animals onboard, you'll need to comply with the provisions of SABRE (Safe Animal Breeding in Restricted Environments). Lastly, PFO (Poo-Free Oceans) is keen to know about your animal waste disposal plans. After all, no one wants to see the ocean develop a great poo patch that continuously floats around.

Yours,

Benjamin Dan
Senior Safety Officer

DISCUSSION

THE REASON FOR THE FLOOD

It is unclear exactly why God brought a flood at this point in history, although the level of corruption and violence on the earth clearly played a role. Some commentators suggest the presence of the mysterious Nephilim[6] (Genesis 6:4) was also a significant factor.

ANIMAL LOGISTICS

Contrary to popular belief, there were more than two of each kind of animal on the ark.

> *Take with you seven pairs of every kind of clean animal, a male and its mate, and one pair of every kind of unclean animal, a male and its mate, and also seven pairs of every kind of bird, male and female, to keep their various kinds alive throughout the earth.*
>
> *Genesis 7:2-3*

God supernaturally sent animals directly to the ark, which must have been a real time saver for Noah (Genesis 7:8-10). Many of the physically larger animals may have been taken on as juveniles, not only saving on space but reducing food requirements and making handling easier. Juveniles would also have the advantage of living longer and having more remaining reproductive years than older adults.

BEHIND CLOSED DOORS

Conversations we never heard but might have happened:

"Did someone leave the door open on the lion cage, because we now have three fewer zebras?"

"Has anyone watered the otters? Their fur's looking very dry and ruffled."

"The elephant pen needs cleaning. Their diarrhoea's back, and I did it last time."

"Don't go down to level three, the skunks are obviously upset about something."

WHERE DID THE FLOODWATER GO?

Many people have wondered where all the water went after the flood. Scripture suggests there was a post-flood reshaping of the earth's surface with some land sinking and forming basins, and other parts rising. If so, it would mean most of the floodwater remained on the earth's surface. Some of the water may have ended up as polar ice or giant glaciers that formed in a post-flood world under a different climate, or it returned below the earth's surface.

---

6   Numerous theories have been put forward to explain who these beings were, from the mundane, to theories linking them to the gods recorded in Greek mythology. If you go digging into this subject, don't say I didn't warn you! You might be about to enter the Christian version of the twilight zone.

> *He set the earth on its foundations; it can never be moved. You covered it with the watery depths as with a garment; the waters stood above the mountains. But at your rebuke the waters fled, at the sound of your thunder they took to flight; they flowed over the mountains, they went down into the valleys, to the place you assigned for them.*
>
> *Psalm 104:5-8*

Some water could also have pooled into giant lakes which have since vanished or shrunk. Thousands of years ago, Lake Chad in Africa was estimated to have covered 400,000 square kilometres,[7] making it larger than Germany, yet measurements from 2020 indicate it is now closer to 1,540 square kilometres in size.

CULTURAL KNOWLEDGE OF THE FLOOD

Once they left the ark, people stayed together for a hundred years, until the tower of Babel incident resulted in them going their separate ways (Genesis 11:1-9). During this time, Noah's descendants would have picked up two things:

(1) Knowledge of the flood event

(2) Knowledge of the God of Genesis

Many cultures around the world retain a flood story in their history.[8] The Māori people of New Zealand tell of an ancestor, Māui, fishing up land from the ocean, which could be interpreted as land appearing from a flooded earth. Even cultures who believe in many gods often recognise the existence of one God who is superior to all the others. Some Māori talk of Io (Io Matua Kore), a God without parents and all powerful. For many centuries, until 1911, the imperial Chinese emperor made an annual 'border sacrifice' to a supreme being, Shangdi.[9]

THE ARK'S LOCATION

After floating for months, the ark came to rest on the mountains of Ararat (Genesis 8:3-4). Some take this as being Mt. Ararat in Turkey, while others understand it to be a mountain in the Ararat region. Mt. Ararat has a base nearly 35 kilometres wide, and two volcanic cones (peaks) around 11 kilometres apart—Lesser Ararat (3896m) and Greater Ararat (5137m). The ark could have rested on either; or, it may have perished, been buried under ice, been located on a different mountain entirely, or perhaps Noah and his descendants used its wood for building other structures and for fuel. An ark-shaped anomaly has been identified on Mt. Ararat, but despite speculation, no firm evidence has emerged confirming it to be Noah's ark.[10]

7   www.earthobservatory.nasa.gov/images/146304/remnants-of-an-ancient-lake

8   https//en.wikipedia.org/wiki/List_of_flood_myths

9   www.answersingenesis.org/genesis/the-original-unknown-god-of-china

10 www.icr.org/article/did-someone-really-find-noahs-ark

THE PROBLEM OF SIN

God may have wiped out sinners in a flood, but sin still lurked deep in the human heart—even within Noah who was said to have been a righteous man (Genesis 6:9). It didn't take long for humanity's new beginning to unravel. Noah planted a vineyard and made wine (good), then got drunk and naked (bad). A mysterious event followed (very bad), resulting in Noah pronouncing a curse on some of his unborn descendants (Genesis 9:20-25). God didn't end up with sin-free people, even when he got the population down to only eight humans. Removing almost everyone wasn't the solution to the sin problem—something different was called for.

MOSES AND HIS RED SEA PROBLEM

Cohen, Stern & Steinbach
Egyptian Branch Office
Pyramid Row

Moses
Burning Bush Hotel
Egypt

Date: Reign of Ramesses II

Dear Moses,

Despite the kind hospitality Pharaoh extended to your people over many years, I understand they recently made a rather hasty departure from his country, leaving behind an unresolved labour dispute involving brickmaking.

There is also an accusation (false, I'm sure) that you were personally involved in some way with a multitude of recent plagues upon the land. Across my desk have come tales of an excess of frogs, hail, and a swarm of locusts of truly biblical proportions. A particular favourite of mine was when the water in the Nile turned to blood—a little unpleasant for those who happened to be taking swimming lessons that day. The final plague, involving the death of first-born people and animals, was clearly overdoing it though. If it turns out you *were* connected with that one, then shoddy brickmaking and a blood-filled Nile will be the least of your worries.

One thing I can tell you is that the nation's wheat farmers are planning a class action against whoever is responsible for all those locusts. I'm not saying you had any involvement, you understand, but in my experience it usually works out cheaper for the guilty party if they settle out of court. As one might imagine, the pollution unit of the local council isn't happy about the state of the Nile either, and they are looking for someone to hold responsible for killing the fish.

Speaking of dead fish, rumour has it you currently face the predicament of how to transport your several million followers across the Red Sea. I'm guessing your desire to cross over as soon as possible may have something to do with the imminent arrival of the Egyptian army at your current location. What's that old Egyptian proverb, "A half-made brick returns no favours?"

Fortunately for you, Cohen, Stern & Steinbach have taken the initiative and investigated two transport options for your consideration. A bridge could be constructed, which would keep your feet dry during the crossing in accordance with your preference. Regrettably, bridges aren't cheap to build and involve complex engineering. The last thing anyone wants is for the designer to miss something and the bridge to unexpectedly start swaying violently from side to side as people walk across it on opening day.[11]

You may therefore favour the alternative solution offered by Jordan Coastal Shipping and Freight Company. They are first-class purveyors of water-based transportation logistics and can provide you with a fleet of suitable vessels at short notice. Each would come with an experienced captain and crew, all for a very competitive daily rate. Choose them, and they will have you, your people and any freight on the other side of the Red Sea in virtually no time at all. All I require is a signed contract and a deposit, with the remaining balance to be received within seven days of the last person disembarking. The deal also includes full insurance by Lloyds Skiffs.

I've come across a few wild stories in my time, but expecting *God* to part the waters of the Red Sea to provide you with dry land to cross over on . . . well, let me just say,

---

11 On the 10th of June 2000, the 325-metre-long suspension style Millennium Bridge across London's river Thames first opened to foot traffic. However, it soon developed an intense side-to-side wobble, and the bridge was closed pending an investigation.

it's a story that hopefully will make its way into a best-selling book someday. It's an absolutely fantastic tale, but seriously, I do strongly suggest (especially in light of Pharaoh's somewhat volatile temperament) that you avail yourself of the services of Jordan Coastal Shipping without further delay, unless you want to take your chances waiting for a bridge to be built.

Even if you should all make it across the Red Sea by other means—and I don't want to sound sceptical but that does seem somewhat unlikely—you'll be facing a difficult desert environment. The good news is that Cohen, Stern, & Steinbach have a staff member based in the area—a Mr T. E. Lawrence.[12] If required, he can put you in contact with suppliers of dates, camels, salt merchants, and even well diggers. Choose to work with Cohen, Stern & Steinbach and you'll quickly appreciate the benefits of dealing with an established, reputable company that charges modest fees for excellent levels of service.

Yours,

Arron Cohen
Cohen, Stern & Steinbach

---

12 T.E. Lawrence (1888–1935). Known also as *Lawrence of Arabia*

DISCUSSION

HOW IT ALL BEGAN

The story of Moses and the crossing of the Red Sea began around four hundred years earlier with the arrival in Egypt of a man called Joseph. Demonstrating his capability by saving the nation from the effects of a long famine, his family was allowed to immigrate to the land. As years passed, his family group (the Hebrews or Israelites) became very numerous, and eventually, the day came when the story of Joseph's contribution to the nation became forgotten (Exodus1:8).

FROM CAPTIVITY TO FREEDOM

The Israelites eventually fell out of favour and were put to work as slaves making bricks (Exodus 1:8-14), a job that became harder when they had to collect their own straw instead of having it supplied (Exodus 5:6-8). One day, God appeared to Moses from a burning bush (Exodus 3:1-10) and appointed him to lead the Israelites from captivity in Egypt to freedom. Jesus offers us the same deal. If we trust him with our life, he can lead us out of our captivity, brokenness and disappointment into something new.

THE PLAGUES OF EGYPT

Understandably, Pharaoh wasn't too keen on losing all that free labour and told Moses the brickmakers were staying put. Moses and his brother, Aaron, did some cool tricks involving a stick and a snake, but Pharaoh's court magicians were able to replicate the trick (Exodus 7:8-12). Next, when Moses waved his staff and the Nile turned to blood, Pharaoh's magicians did the same thing. Sometimes, as these examples show, demonic power can mimic the things of God.

A week later, with the brickmakers still not going anywhere, Moses waved his hand and, *hey presto,* an excess of frogs appeared. The magicians did likewise, and suddenly there was an excessive excess of frogs. Next up, gnats—but the magicians had met their match and couldn't produce their own gnats (although why you'd want gnats on top of gnats is anyone's guess). Despite recovering from a double helping of frogs, blood, and being surrounded on all sides by gnats, Pharaoh still said the brickmakers weren't going anywhere. Plagues of flies, the death of livestock, boils, hail, locusts and darkness followed. (I'm imagining Egyptian tourism was suffering a downturn by this point.) Finally came the death of the first born—both people and animals.

A GOD OF RESCUE

Pharaoh, now out of options and with reduced livestock figures, finally relented and said the Israelites could leave. So off they went, and all was well . . . that is, until Pharaoh changed his mind again and wanted his brickmakers back.

> When the king of Egypt was told that the people had fled, Pharaoh and his officials changed their minds about them and said, "What have we done? We have let the Israelites go and have lost their services!"
>
> Exodus 14:5

Pharaoh dispatched the Egyptian army to retrieve them, and suddenly things turned desperate for Moses. He had the Red Sea in front of him and the Egyptian army approaching from behind. Adding to his problems, the people were complaining and fearful (Exodus 14:11-12). Yet just when the situation looked completely hopeless, God miraculously parted the Red Sea and the Hebrews crossed over to safety. When the Egyptian army tried to follow, the water quickly returned and drowned them.

Have you ever found yourself in a Moses situation? Something prevents you from moving forward, while at the same time, something from the past grows larger, threatening to overwhelm you. Whatever your combination of circumstances, God stands ready to help. In fact, often we only need to stand still and allow God to do the heaving lifting. Such was the case for the Israelites against the Egyptian army.

> Moses answered the people, "Do not be afraid. Stand firm and you will see the deliverance the Lord will bring you today. The Egyptians you see today you will never see again. The Lord will fight for you; you need only to be still."
>
> Exodus 14:13-14

Deliverance from difficult or dire situations isn't reserved only for biblical characters. God is still in the rescue business today. When things have become difficult, your way forward is blocked and an army of undesirable circumstances are advancing on you, you too can call out to God and ask him to provide you with a dry path through any situation.

THE WONDERFUL WALL OF JERICHO CITY

Superior Walls & Fortifications (SWF) Ltd
Industrial Precinct
Cana

The Mayor
Jericho City
Jericho

Date: 1406 B.C.

Dear Mr Mayor,

Yesterday, Jericho's Clerk of Works burst into my office gasping for air like a man having a heart attack. Once calmer and able to talk, he informed me you were most concerned about the hordes of riffraff who have recently turned up from across the Jordan River.

Do not concern yourself, Mr Mayor. These people are no more than nomadic Jewish desert wanderers—failed brickmakers at best. Since leaving Egypt decades ago they have wandered aimlessly in the desert, doing little more than developing an unhealthy obsession with eating manna and dropping dead. Their only claim to fame (if one can even call it that) is successfully escaping from the Egyptian army—although 'escape' might be overstating it. (The unlucky Egyptians got caught out on an unusually rapid incoming tide and drowned.) Recently, their leader—a one-time cattle herder called Moses—died and was buried who knows where, and Joshua has taken over.

It has been observed that their clothing is terribly out of date, almost as though they haven't updated their wardrobes in forty years. Imagine not buying any new clothes for four decades—my wife would be distraught! She'd no longer be able to claim that a dress bought a few years ago had 'worn out' or that her expensive five-year-old jacket had gone 'out of fashion'. Without her clothes to keep paying for, however, I might finally be able to save enough to afford that new sports chariot I've had my eye on—the one in red with racing stripes and a set of white-walled wheels.

I've digressed a little, but rest assured your fears are without foundation, unlike your city wall which has excellent foundations. Superior Walls & Fortifications put their heart and soul into constructing your wall, and it remains the most impressive one around these parts. If you want my advice, your focus shouldn't be on the scruffy homeless people outside the wall but on those who live inside it—the sort of person who might lack loyalty and be prepared to help out an enemy, for example. It might interest you to know that a survey in the Canaanite Sociology Journal (Issue LXII) found that 'women of the night' are the ones most likely to reveal city secrets to others.

My cousin Uri (an intelligence officer in the Egyptian army) recently informed me that this desert-wandering group of Israelites has some sort of magic box they move around using long wooden poles.[13] Why they don't fit it with handles like normal people is anyone's guess. Then again, normal people also update their clothes far more often. The box is known as the Ark of the Covenant, but its contents and function remain unknown. Uri suggested it might be some sort of alien technology supplied by those who built the pyramids. Admittedly, that was after he'd had three bottles of wine. While still sober, he did say that should the Israelites start carrying the ark around your city with men dressed in white linen walking out in front blowing trumpets, leave quickly. When pressed for details, he claimed he'd already said too much. It's just an old box, so personally, I wouldn't worry about it. You could blast an orchestra's worth of trumpets at our wall without anything happening to it—that I can absolutely promise you.

Yours,

Eli Hoffman
Managing Director

---

13 Exodus 25:10-16. The ark was moved by priests using wooden poles.

DISCUSSION

A NEW GENERATION

After hundreds of years as slaves, the Israelites escaped Egypt, crossed the Red Sea, and began their journey to the promised land.[14] Upon their arrival in the desert, God ordered a group of men to go and spy on the land before invading it. Ten of the twelve spies reported back, "It's too hard; it can't be done." However, the remaining two spies—Joshua and Caleb—thought differently. "Piece of cake," they said. "We can do it with one hand tied behind our backs" (Numbers 13:27-33). Alas, the people believed the ten and grumbled against God. As punishment, they had to wander the desert for forty years—one year for every day the spies were away (Numbers 14:26-35). Finally, the day came when all the grumblers were dead; only Joshua and Caleb (the two 'good' spies) remained from the older generation. After the death of Moses, Joshua took over as leader. A new generation had dawned.

Life can be full of major and uncomfortable changes. At some point, we will all find ourselves having to adapt to something new—living in a new city or country, welcoming our first baby, or starting a new job for example. If you find yourself in this situation, allow these words from Joshua 3:4 (delivered just before the Israelites crossed the Jordan River into their new home) to speak to your heart: "Then you will know which way to go, since you have never been this way before."

JOSHUA'S FIRST TEST

Joshua was a yet unproven leader. His first task was to cross the flooded Jordan River—likely several hundred metres wide at the time. He ordered a group of priests to carry the Ark of the Covenant into the flood waters, knowing that if God didn't come through for them, death by drowning was a distinct possibility. Everyone else was commanded to stay back, way back—2000 cubits (or roughly 900 metres) back, to be precise (Joshua 3:4).

WHAT THE PRIESTS REALLY THOUGHT

"Do you trust him . . . you know, Joshua?"

"Not sure. I trusted Moses, but he's dead, and soon we might be too."

"Why is everyone standing so far away?"

"Joshua probably doesn't want them to see us drown."

"I've got a bad feeling about this."

"Did you say we're going to drown? Oh, woe is me, why did I become a priest?"

"My feet are getting wet, we're doomed—doomed, I tell you."

"Hey, the river's stopped flowing, we're saved—saved, I tell you."

---

14   God had promised land to their ancestors (Genesis 12:1,7).

"I knew we'd be fine, never doubted it for a moment."

A SAFE CROSSING

As promised, God stopped the flow of the Jordan River and the Israelites crossed over safely to the plains of Jericho. At this point, there was a change back to the natural order of things: The manna stopped appearing daily, and the people's clothing, which was previously sustained by God (Deuteronomy 29:5), began to wear out.

THE ROLE OF RAHAB

Joshua's next job was to take over the city of Jericho. There was only one small problem—it was surrounded by a defensive wall. Two spies were sent in and met up with a woman named Rahab (described as a harlot in some translations) who lived inside the thick city wall. She agreed to provide them with bed and breakfast in exchange for sparing her life and the lives of her family when the invasion came (Joshua 2:12-21). Rahab later married Salmon, and her descendants included King David. In this story, we see God's love reaching out to a foreign Canaanite sex-worker in a city marked for destruction. Her life is a beautiful example of how God can redeem a person's past and give them a new future.

Rahab was commended for her actions in helping the spies (Hebrews 11:31), but the question remains: Was she a traitor or a hero? It is a matter of perspective. During World War II, Dietrich Bonhoeffer[15] went against Hitler's national military plans for Germany. We could ask a similar question of him. Was he a traitor to the nation, or a hero for humanity?

THE FALL OF JERICHO

The invasion plan involved the Israelites walking daily around Jericho for six days, and on the seventh day walking around it seven times—a total of thirteen laps. One can only imagine the psychological effect on the residents when, on day seven, the Israelites begin a second lap. The Ark of the Covenant was carried on each lap of the city to the sound of trumpets. After the final lap, Joshua commanded the army to give a loud shout, and the wall fell (Joshua 6:1-27).

Whatever walls we face—no matter how thick, unclimbable, or seemingly immovable they are—God has a plan for getting us through them. Sometimes the walls are not physically in front of us but around our heart. We have built them ourselves because of previous hurt, disappointment, loss, grief, or betrayal. When we wall off our hearts and emotions, it becomes harder for us to relate to others, and for God

---

15 Dietrich Bonhoeffer (1906-1945) was a German Lutheran pastor who became an anti-Nazi dissident. His job in the Abwehr (military intelligence) allowed him to travel overseas where he passed on information to the Allies. On Hitler's personal orders, he was executed at Flossenbürg concentration camp on the 9th April 1945. Germany surrendered on 7th May, 1945.

to relate to us. It will be difficult, and perhaps painful, but I encourage you to ask God to start breaking down the walls around your heart so he can bring you into a place of greater freedom and growth.

DELILAH TO THE ROPE COMPANY

Delilah
Vineyard Road
Sorek Estate

The Philistinian Rope & Twine Company
Gath Industrial Estate

Date: 1120 B.C.

Dear Sir,

I recently visited your store to buy rope. The rope was required so I could undertake a very important task on behalf of the government. I explained how the rope needed to be strong, very strong. The young salesman listened to my request with all the enthusiasm of a person watching paint dry. Randomly pulling something akin to twine from a nearby reel he turned and said, "This will do it." I explained to him a second time that I needed the strongest rope available. He sighed heavily, lowered his chin to his chest and with feet dragging along the floor, shuffled reluctantly over to a spool labelled, *"Super* Rope". "It's the strongest you can get," he mumbled. What he lacked in enthusiasm he made up for in body odour.

To make sure he truly understood the importance of the rope needing to be strong, I explained it was to be used in tying up a dangerous criminal before they were taken into custody. "Ten men couldn't break this rope," he boasted as he finished winding it up and taking my money.

The man in question was secured with your so called *"Super* Rope". Job done—or so it looked. Moments after becoming aware that he'd been restrained, the man broke free as if the rope was nothing stronger than sewing thread.

Fortunately, the men who were to take the criminal into custody hadn't moved in to make the arrest. Should they have done so, I expect they would have ended up as shredded as the rope was. Are you certain I was sold new rope? Seeing how poorly it performed, I'm wondering if what I was sold was actually second-rate rope. Or maybe second-hand rope that your less-than-helpful sales assistant had wound onto an empty spool that had a *"Super* Rope" sticker on it? I've heard of stores that palm off used rope to unwary customers. Is yours one of those stores? Or maybe the rope I purchased had been left sitting outside in the storage yard, in the rain and damp, deteriorating and weakening by the day.

Since this incident, I have found out that soldiers from the Israelite army tied up the same man with ropes, which he also broke free from. One can't help but think there is a lot of faulty rope currently being sold. I am extremely disappointed that this rope, *far* more expensive than any other you sell, failed so quickly. This has caused a serious delay in bringing this wanted man into custody, and you can be certain my superiors will be contacting you. I have also passed on the name of the salesman. (I was going to say the salesman who "helped me" but that would be overstating things.) I've suggested to my superiors that you'd both be ideal candidates to try out the new hangman knots on. I believe the trials start next week.

To be honest, I don't think this rope contains anything 'super' at all, just like dog biscuits don't contain dog, and cat biscuits don't contain any cat. Instead of offering superior performance, the *"Super"* name is clearly nothing more than a marketing gimmick used to scam a few more shekels out of people who can't tell packaging twine from anchor rope. I will call in next Wednesday and I will expect to collect nothing less than a full refund of the purchase price.

Yours,

Delilah

DISCUSSION

The story of Samson, the strong man who gets tied up, is found in the book of Judges, chapters thirteen to sixteen. It is another story of a man behaving badly and allowing a woman to draw him away from the things of God. Samson and King David both allowed a forbidden relationship with a woman to negatively impact their walk with God.

This isn't to say that women can't be led astray by men or behave badly; they can. It's just that the Bible has more 'men behaving badly' stories between its pages. That said, Jezebel arranged a murder to obtain her husband a vineyard (1 Kings 21:1–16). The daughter of Herodias asked for the head of John the Baptist on a platter and got it (Matthew 14:6–11). There are others, too, if you go looking for them.

But back to Samson. In Samson's case, he became involved with Delilah. It wasn't an ideal thing for him to have done as she wasn't Jewish. Rather, she was a Philistine and worshipped foreign gods and not the God of Israel. In the New Testament, we are given a warning concerning unequal spiritual pairings involving marriage:

> *Do not be yoked together with unbelievers. For what do righteousness and wickedness have in common? Or what fellowship can light have with darkness?*
>
> *2 Corinthians 6:14*

SPIRITUAL DIFFERENCES IN MARRIAGE

When two Christians marry, they share a common faith and a common spiritual understanding. If one is a non-Christian, spiritual differences can lead to spiritual tension or a desire to do things in different ways, for example, how children will be raised. They may also have differing boundaries and differing views on morality.

That said—although a special situation—Esther married the non-Jewish king Xerxes[16] of Persia, who was a Mede by descent (Daniel 9:1). He wasn't Jewish like Esther was, and he didn't grow up worshipping Esther's God. Paul makes this comment about spiritual unevenness involving marriage in 1 Corinthians 7:14:

---

16 In certain Bible versions, such as the New International Version (NIV), he is referred to as "Xerxes", but as "Ahasuerus" in the English Standard Version (ESV) and others. These sorts of differences arise from different approaches to Bible translation, whether to keep a person's name in the original language or convert it to an English equivalent.

> *For the unbelieving husband has been sanctified through his wife, and the unbelieving wife has been sanctified through her believing husband. Otherwise your children would be unclean, but as it is, they are holy.*

In talking about the unbeliever being sanctified, Paul is not endorsing the idea of a Christian marrying an unbeliever. He was letting the Christian know that they and any of their children would not be made spiritually unclean by the unbelieving partner.

In Genesis 18:24-26, Abraham was pleading with God to spare Sodom if fifty righteous people lived there. God agreed, showing that his 'blessing' of not being destroyed would come to all the unbelievers who lived there because of those believers who did. Unfortunately, there weren't even ten believers and the place got turned into an ash heap. But the principle is that God's blessing can flow through the believer to the family, even though they are married to an unbeliever.

SAMSON'S COMPROMISES

Nowhere does the Bible indicate that Samson married Delilah, but in maintaining the relationship, Samson was led to make compromises in his life. A similar situation arose for King Solomon, the son of King David, who "loved many foreign women" (1 Kings 11:1). God had warned Israelite men against marrying foreign women, as it would lead to their hearts being turned towards other gods (1 Kings 11:2). Samson ended up revealing the secret of his God-given strength—his uncut hair. When it was cut, he lost his superhuman strength, allowing him to be subdued and tied up. His eyes were poked out, leaving him to be little more than a performing monkey at the hands of the Philistines.

SAMSON'S FAITH IN GOD

Despite being in a weakened and blind state, Samson eventually reconnected with God and slowly regained his superhuman strength. This allowed him to wipe out a large number of Philistines in one final act (Judges 16:28–30). One could say he brought the house down or in this case, brought a pagan Philistine temple down, one that just happened to have thousands of Philistines inside. Samson gets a mention in the New Testament in the book of Hebrews as a hero of the faith (Hebrews 11:32).

In Samson, we see a picture of a person whose lifestyle and choices led them away from God and their calling. Yet we also see the love of God keeping the door open, up to the last minute, so Samson, despite his history of sin, could find his way back into the relationship. The major risk of being away from God and out of relationship with him is that even though it is possible to make a last-minute return as Samson did, a person never knows when their last minute will be.

AN ALMOST DEFEATED ARMY

Arrow Systems Corporation
Weapons Specialists
Military Industrial Complex

Abner
Commander in Chief
Israelite Army

Date: 1025 B.C.

Dear Abner,

Congratulations on your recent victory over the Philistines at the valley of Elah. It's about time someone showed them who's boss around these parts!

I am told there was a Philistine giant called Goliath who came out each morning to challenge your army to fight—and caused your soldiers to rush to the latrines, placing an unhealthy demand on the supplies of toilet paper. If the descriptions I've heard about him (including being nine feet tall) are true, I can understand your soldiers being reluctant to engage with him.

Nevertheless, army life isn't all about visiting the mess tent, helping out after disasters, and guarding plague centres to stop people escaping. The time comes when one must actually fight. Is it true that Goliath's daily 'winner takes all' challenge went unmet for forty days? I think you'll agree that any army unwilling to take on the enemy for that length of time could use some help—help that Arrow Systems Corporation stands ready to supply.

I'm all for performance bonuses being offered by the king. However, a lump sum along with a permanent tax exemption for the soldier and his family, and the hand of the king's daughter in marriage for the soldier who killed Goliath, struck me as quite excessive. Yet, this burst of generosity still failed to motivate a single soldier to attack Goliath? Not a good look for a professional fighting force, is it now? What if the army is called upon to tackle more of these Goliath-sized challenges? Will the king keep making similar offers until he runs out of daughters to give away?

According to my sources, Goliath wasn't even killed by one of your regular soldiers, but by a young shepherd called David who just so happened to have turned up to visit his brothers. It's quite remarkable really—a youth armed with a slingshot and a few river stones taking on a giant enemy soldier; it's a miracle the boy lived. I'm certain your army would feel far more confident meeting these modern combat situations equipped with the latest military hardware—Arrow Systems Corporation military hardware.

I'd like to extend an invitation for you to attend the Sword and Shield Expo next month where Arrow Systems will be demonstrating our latest products—all of which carry the military trademark (MTM). You'll be able to test out our 4Eva-Sharp[MTM] blade and tip technology and ride a few circuits around the track on a Speedy-Wheels[MTM] combat chariot. You could even win a weekend for two if you can hit the bullseye with a FlyFAR[MTM] spear or javelin, or with an arrow fired from an ArrowBOOST[MTM] archery bow. I hear David was offered King Saul's armour to wear but it was too large for him. Well, problem solved, as our new Strike-SAFE[MTM] armour comes in a range of sizes better suited to the smaller soldier.

I sense the winds of change are blowing, so now would be a good time to arm your forces and prepare for what lies ahead.

Yours,

Ehud Finkelstein
New Weapons Manager

DISCUSSION

THE GIANTS WE FACE

Do you have a 'Goliath' in your life? Many of us do. The giants we face can be people—a workplace bully, for example—or addictions, sexual sin, financial issues, or maybe even prior abuse. Giants are intimidating; they keep coming back time and again unless they are killed. Goliath was relentless too, tormenting the Israelite army every morning for forty days. Although they were better armed and protected than David, Israel's soldiers were still not confident enough to take him on.

We too may feel ill-equipped to take on the giant in our life. Fortunately, God takes what little we can offer him and works with that. David turned up with five stones but only had to use one. Ultimately, David placed his faith in God. Goliath saw David as an enemy he could beat; David saw Goliath as an enemy God could beat. Even if all we can offer God is our faith and obedience, when it comes to defeating our giants, those two things are enough.

A CHALLENGING PATH TO VICTORY

As with many issues in life, the path to achieving victory over our giants is generally not a smooth one. Before David even got the chance to swing his sling, he faced opposition from his own family. His brother Eliab lashed out at him with a list of false complaints including abandoning the sheep and only showing up to be a spectator (1 Samuel 17:28).

Embarking on major personal change may cause others to rise up against you. Walking away from sin or a sinful lifestyle always causes disruption. Converting to Christianity can cause even more. Sometimes, our enemies can include those from within our own household (Matthew 10:36). Even Jesus was betrayed by one of his disciples (Judas Iscariot), and on another occasion, his own family cast doubts on his sanity (Mark 3:21).

THE UNSEEN SPIRITUAL BATTLE

As David walked out to confront Goliath, he placed his reliance on God rather than on his slingshot or his previous experience as a shepherd defending his sheep against wild animals.

> David said to the Philistine, "You come against me with sword and spear and javelin, but I come against you in the name of the Lord Almighty, the God of the armies of Israel, whom you have defied."
>
> *1 Samuel 17:45*

Of all the weapons one could choose, the name of the Lord spoken in faith is by far the most powerful. Although David confronted a physical enemy with a slingshot, the real battle was occurring behind the scenes in the invisible realm, something Paul highlights multiple times in Scripture:

> *For our struggle is not against flesh and blood, but against the rulers, against the authorities, against the powers of this dark world and against the spiritual forces of evil in the heavenly realms.*
>
> *Ephesians 6:12*

> *For though we live in the world, we do not wage war as the world does. The weapons we fight with are not the weapons of the world. On the contrary, they have divine power to demolish strongholds.*
>
> *2 Corinthians 10:3-4*

We need to keep in mind that the giants we see with our eyes are often being driven and influenced by unseen dark powers. The physical weapons of the world are ineffective in spiritual battles, but fortunately, God has given us spiritual weapons with which to fight. One of these was used by David: *the name of the Lord Almighty*. In David's case, the battle was won in the spiritual realm first, then the physical realm.

THE VALUE OF THE OLD TESTAMENT

The David vs. Goliath story is found in the Old Testament, a part of the Bible many consider to be 'full of boring stuff'. While it's true that Leviticus and Deuteronomy can be a slog to read, Bible stories still speak to modern hearts and lives. Understood in its entirety, the Bible accurately describes the state of the world and how the people living in it should conduct themselves. Even in our modern world, bad behaviour hasn't changed. There is nothing new when it comes to sin and human behaviour (Ecclesiastes 1:9).

The Old Testament is full of stories involving faith and doubt, adultery, political scandals, murder, and kings who worship the wrong gods. There's a beauty contest (Esther 2:2-4), a set of giant gallows (Esther 7:9), a talking donkey (Numbers 22:27-30), a prophet preaching naked for three years (Isaiah 20:1-4),[17] and another prophet who had to lie on his side for 430 days (bed sores anyone?).[18] There's a jar of oil that doesn't run out (1 Kings 17:16), a prophet fed with meat delivered by birds (1 Kings 17:1-6), and an outbreak of deadly snakes (Numbers 21:4-9).

As with the story of David and Goliath, the Old Testament has much to teach those who take the time to read it. It may be historical in nature, but for the Christian, it is history that is worth reading (Romans 15:4).

---

17 There is some debate as to whether he was totally naked or only wore the equivalent of underpants.

18 Ezekiel 4:1-8. He lay for 390 days on his left side, had a quick stretch, then lay for 40 days on his right side.

850 DEAD PROPHETS

Samaria Police Department
District Four
DCI Berman

Mr Elijah
Prophet of God
School of the Prophets

Date: 860 B.C.

Category:	Criminal—Mass Murder?
Event:	Deaths of Prophets of Baal and Asherah
Location:	Kishon Valley
Case Number:	C28649/091

Dear Sir,

Officers from this district recently attended a major harm incident where the bodies of 850 deceased males were discovered: 450 prophets of the god Baal and 400 prophets of the god Asherah. Events appear to have centred around two altars: one was still fully intact with an untouched sacrifice, and the second was a pile of scorched earth.

Police are currently working to determine the sequence of events, and your name has been mentioned by numerous eyewitnesses. Our sources indicate that on the day in question, you were holding a 'my God is more real than your god' challenge, and when the challenge ended, those belonging to the losing side were killed.

Normally you would have been brought in for questioning by now, but details supplied by those present have raised serious issues involving the credibility of their testimonies.

Furthermore, it is understood the deceased prophets voluntarily participated in the challenge and agreed to the terms and conditions. That said, we remain uncertain whether the losing side was aware they would be killed if they lost. Specifically, the claims I am finding difficult to substantiate are as follows:

1. You obtained a significant amount of water three years into a drought.

2. You caused the multitude of injuries to the Baal prophets. It seems far more likely they cut themselves with swords and spears and, therefore, may be responsible for their own deaths from blood loss and/or shock. In a nutshell, they committed a form of ritualistic group suicide. As the 'event' occurred on a sunny day, it is also possible that some, if not indeed the majority, died from some combination of exhaustion, heatstroke, or dehydration. It's difficult to believe they stood wailing to their god for hours upon end under the noon-day sun just because you told them to. If this was indeed the case, the cause of death—excessive sunshine—would once again be self-inflicted. Nevertheless, this will be a matter for the coroner to decide, and with 850 bodies to autopsy, he's going to be a busy man indeed.

3. You caused lightning to fall from a clear blue sky. This one I found particularly difficult to accept—as did the police consultant meteorologist. There is that old saying, "a bolt from the blue," so the lightning bolt theory hasn't entirely been discounted. However, it doesn't appear the prophets were actually killed by lightning, so this isn't a priority item. It also seems dubious that a sacrificial altar made of stone was completely melted. No doubt it would be connected to the 'bolt from the blue' mentioned above, but needless to say, it's also not a crime.

4. You caused torrential rain to fall resulting in a major flooding event that ended the drought. We have good evidence for the rain and flood, but as for you causing it—it's doubtful. At this point, the prophets were already dead, so this relates more to the credibility of eyewitnesses than your possible guilt. There has, however, been a complaint by the local council concerning an 'unconsented discharge of water' in breach of the Water Resources Management Act, section IV. That's the council for you—complains when there's a drought, complains when it comes to an end.

Relatives of some of the deceased have filed a complaint with the Religious Relations Board here in Samaria. They claim you insulted their god Baal, by saying he was inattentive, sleeping on the job, busy with other things, or even going to the toilet.[19] If this is true, your statements may well constitute religious hate speech under current legislative interpretations. Fortunately for you, this has yet to be tested in court, although I'm sure the day will come.

To assist us in our ongoing investigation, I request you contact this station to arrange a suitable time to come in and make a formal statement regarding your involvement in these matters.

Yours,

Detective Chief Inspector Berman

---

19 Several Bible translations directly mention Baal using a toilet e.g., The Living Bible (TLB) and the Contemporary English Version (CEV). Others like the English Standard Version (ESV) suggest it indirectly with the phrase "relieving himself."

DISCUSSION

> *There was never anyone like Ahab, who sold himself to do evil in the eyes of the Lord, urged on by Jezebel his wife.*
>
> *1 Kings 21:25*

A WEAKNESS FOR IDOL WORSHIP

So, what led to the showdown between Elijah and the false prophets? In the Old Testament, God's children were commanded not to worship false gods or idols (Leviticus 19:4). Idols, of course, aren't true gods[20] (Isaiah 45:20; Psalm 135:15-18, 115:4-8) but rather fancy wood-carving projects. They can also be made from stone as many of the Egyptian gods were, or cast from molten metal. The children of Israel actually did this while Moses was on Mt. Sinai receiving the ten commandments. They melted down their earrings and made themselves a golden calf which they then proceeded to worship (Exodus 32:1-5).

Much later, King Ahab of Israel married Jezebel (the daughter of a foreign king) and soon began to serve and worship the false gods of her culture. If Ahab was bad, Jezebel was very much the power behind Ahab's throne. She killed off God's prophets (1 Kings 18:4) and replaced them with an army of her own—850 prophets of Baal and Asherah. The Bible does not speak kindly of King Ahab:

GOD INTERVENES THROUGH ELIJAH

When the land was in its third year of drought—an act of judgement due to King Ahab's actions (1 Kings 17:1)—God told Elijah to go and see King Ahab. Elijah did so, and proceeded to tell the king he'd been a bad boy:

> *"I have not made trouble for Israel," Elijah replied. "But you and your father's family have. You have abandoned the Lord's commands and have followed the Baals. Now summon the people from all over Israel to meet me on Mount Carmel. And bring the four hundred and fifty prophets of Baal and the four hundred prophets of Asherah, who eat at Jezebel's table."*
>
> *1 Kings 18:18-19*

It was showdown time at Mount Carmel!

---

20 Idols aren't gods. This point is expanded on by Paul in the New Testament: "We know that 'an idol is nothing at all in the world' and that 'there is no God but one'" (1 Corinthians 8:4).

GOD VS. BAAL

Imagine you don't go to church one particular Sunday and later meet up with someone who did. You ask how the service went, and they tell you the following:

"You should have come, it was amazing. This guy Elijah was the guest speaker, and instead of a sermon he held a showdown between himself and 850 false prophets. The prophets shouted, cut their bodies, and left blood stains across the carpet. They made fools of themselves for most of the service, and nothing happened. Then, it was Elijah's turn. He built an altar from stones, added wood and a pile of meat from the church refrigerator that was meant for the men's barbecue, poured on plenty of water, then prayed.

Kapow! A lightning bolt suddenly struck his altar and the whole lot was gone, leaving a huge hole in the stage. As you can imagine, the pastor's not happy about any of it—including the lost meat and the water stains. Luckily the fire alarm didn't go off, unlike that time the Sunday school re-enacted Moses and the burning bush . . .

Anyway, the drum kit caught fire, and all the old people cheered. Then they cheered even louder a week later when the pastor announced it was going to take months to get replacement drums."

In the real version, Elijah prays, God answers, fire falls, and the sacrifice, wood, stones, water, and soil are all consumed (1 Kings 18:38). The people looking on were not only impressed (and probably terrified) but were instantly convinced of the reality of Elijah's God.

> *When all the people saw this, they fell prostrate and cried, "The Lord—he is God! The Lord—he is God!"*
>
> 1 Kings 18:39

Then, acting under the authority of God's law, Elijah arranged for the false prophets to be killed off:

> *But a prophet who presumes to speak in my name anything I have not commanded, or a prophet who speaks in the name of other gods, is to be put to death.*
>
> Deuteronomy 18:20

> *Whoever sacrifices to any god other than the Lord must be destroyed.*
>
> Exodus 22:20

A NASTY END

Perhaps not surprisingly, having led others deep into sin by worshipping false gods, things didn't end well for the royal couple. King Ahab died in battle (1 Kings 22:34-36), and as for his wife Jezebel, she applied makeup, got herself a new hairdo, then three eunuchs came along and threw her from an upstairs window. Next, she was trampled by horses, and a pack of dogs ate most of what was left of her—leaving only her head, hands and feet behind (2 Kings 9:30-37).

Ultimately, worshipping idols cost King Ahab and his wife Jezebel their lives. Even today, many who follow and worship false gods end up paying a high price—if not in this life, then certainly in the next. The Bible clearly states there is only one true God worthy of our worship, and anyone who chooses to bow down to other gods does so at their peril.

A NAUGHTY KING AND 102 DEAD SOLDIERS

King Ahaziah's Palace
Office of Military Affairs
Bodyguard Services

Major Jazel
Media & Publicity Unit
Army HQ

Date: 852 B.C.

Dear Major Jazel,

The king recently fell through the lattice on his balcony and suffered a life-threatening injury. I had already suggested he have it repaired, but you know how he was when it came to spending money on maintenance. Keen to know if he was going to live or die, he sent some servants to consult the god Baal-Zebub in the town of Ekron. Along the way, who should they run into but the prophet Elijah. He told them not to worry about going to Ekron, and instead he gave them the message that the king was going to die. The king was already in a bad mood, and Elijah's message made things much worse.

In response, he dispatched a captain and fifty soldiers to capture Elijah so the two of them could chat things over, nice and friendly like. Oddly, the soldiers never returned. With the tea and scones getting cold, the king sent another captain and fifty more soldiers. They, too, didn't return. Personally, I didn't care about how cold the scones were getting, but I was getting concerned about the missing soldiers. Although he was already down a hundred and two soldiers, the king sent out a third squad who, this time, fortunately returned with Elijah.

The field report written by the third captain described finding the *incinerated* bodies of those who'd gone before him, and yes, you did read that correctly! Scorched and smouldering bones, scraps of charred uniforms and a lingering smell of burnt flesh were all that remained.

Your task, Major, is to write to all the deceased's next of kin as soon as possible. To assist you, I'm sending two palace scribes who hold Top Secret clearance. Attached to my letter is the cover story you are to use—a terrible accident with an experimental weapon . . . tragic deaths . . . the king mourns their loss . . . brave soldiers of the kingdom etc. To prevent the truth getting out, the bodies won't be returned to loved ones. You'll need to explain that due to the nature of the weapon, returning bodies could result in relatives becoming contaminated, risking their own deaths. Mention National Security being at stake and hint that a special medal may be awarded later to the deceased soldiers.

The palace is intending to keep the matter under wraps for the next two days to allow the scene to be cleaned up and the body parts buried. Even though we are maintaining a full media blackout, there have been sightings of reporters from News Of The Kingdom. Report it immediately to the palace guard if you see any of them snooping around.

There is a second and even more pressing matter: *The king is dead.* This is not to be announced or communicated to anyone else at this time; it is for your eyes only. After Elijah was brought back to the palace, he told the king that because he had tried to consult Baal-Zebub and not Elijah's God, the king would die. And die he did. Elijah should be considered dangerous and should not be approached at this time. Arrangements for the king's funeral are currently being made, and I will write to you with further details once they are finalised.

Yours

Commander Hadon
King's Bodyguard

DISCUSSION

UNDERSTANDING THE WAYS OF GOD

Reading the story of King Ahaziah (2 Kings 1:1-16), it can be tempting to think God acted inappropriately by wiping out the soldiers. Yet, we should always start with the foundation that God is completely righteous and just in all his actions, and any explanation in which God doesn't remain both righteous and just should be rejected.

In order to come to a correct understanding of a difficult Bible passage, context is important. Along with context, we need to take into account any previous warnings or prophecies given, any sinful behaviour of those involved, and God's ultimate plans and purposes for a particular individual, nation, or people group. It is also important to keep in mind that life in the Old Testament was lived under a different covenant than the one introduced by Jesus. The old covenant came with different requirements, provisions and punishments, and was centred around the law.

A SERIES OF FATEFUL DECISIONS

King Ahaziah took over from his father, King Ahab (a very bad king), and despite Elijah wiping out 450 prophets of Baal during the time of Ahab, Ahaziah still chose to follow in his father's footsteps.

> He did evil in the eyes of the Lord, because he followed the ways of his father and mother and of Jeroboam son of Nebat, who caused Israel to sin. He served and worshiped Baal and aroused the anger of the Lord, the God of Israel, just as his father had done.
>
> *1 Kings 22:52-53*

Rather than consult God's appointed prophet Elijah, King Ahaziah chose to consult the false god Baal-Zebub.[21] Nevertheless, the servants returned with a rather dire message from Elijah.

> "A man came to meet us," they replied. "And he said to us, 'Go back to the king who sent you and tell him, "This is what the Lord says: Is it because there is no God in Israel that you are sending messengers to consult Baal-Zebub, the god of Ekron? Therefore you will not leave the bed you are lying on. You will certainly die!"'"
>
> *2 Kings 1:6*

Angered by the message, the king sent soldiers to fetch Elijah. Elijah called down

---

21 Beelzebub is an alternative spelling of Baal-Zebub

fire in response, and the score became King Ahaziah: 0, Elijah: 51. At this point, the king could have chosen to respond differently by repenting, worshipping God, and asking for forgiveness. King Manasseh (also very evil—there is no shortage of bad and evil kings in the Old Testament) went off track spiritually too, but he repented and sought God.

> In his distress he sought the favour of the Lord his God and humbled himself greatly before the God of his ancestors. And when he prayed to him, the Lord was moved by his entreaty and listened to his plea.
>
> *2 Chronicles 33:12-13*

King Ahaziah didn't follow King Manasseh's path; he didn't repent and seek God. Instead, still seeing himself as 'the boss', he sent out more soldiers, which only resulted in more charcoal—King Ahaziah: 0, Elijah: 102.

The pecking order was clear: God, God's prophet, King Ahaziah, then everyone else. It was wrong for King Ahaziah to issue the order to fetch Elijah. Elijah subsequently called on God to make his sovereignty known by answering with fire, and fire there was. Evidently, having not learned his lesson, and with little regard for the lives of his soldiers, the king dispatched a third unit.

Even today, innocent people still die because of the sinful decisions and actions of leaders. For example, Adolf Hitler cost millions of Germans their lives when he started World War II with a view to expanding his country's borders.

GOD AS THE ULTIMATE AUTHORITY

The New Testament tells us that "mercy triumphs over judgment" (James 2:13). The third captain appeared to truly believe Elijah was a servant of God, or maybe it was because of the 102 charred bodies he and his men had to walk through to reach him. Either way, he didn't demand that Elijah comply with the king's order but rather pleaded for mercy—which he received.

> So, the king sent a third captain with his fifty men. This third captain went up and fell on his knees before Elijah. "Man of God," he begged, "please have respect for my life and the lives of these fifty men, your servants!"
>
> *2 Kings 1:13*

Some people hold Elijah responsible for the death of the soldiers, yet fire wouldn't have fallen unless God first allowed it. A challenge against Elijah's authority and his words were effectively a challenge against God himself. The king should never have attempted to order Elijah around, and the commanders and soldiers should not have carried out the king's orders. The king may have been in charge of the country, but he failed to recognise that (as is the case with all of us) a higher authority ruled over him. Against the God of the Universe, no king could ever possibly hope to win.

THREE YOUNG MEN AND A VERY HOT FIRE

Babylon Fire Safety Specialists Ltd
Industrial Zone of Babylon

Shadrach, Meshach and Abednego
Foreign Housing Block
Exile Street

Date: Reign of King Nebuchadnezzar

Dear Shadrach, Meshach, and Abednego,

It was truly wonderful to hear that all three of you survived your trip to the king's furnace—you are the only people to have ever done so. Even allowing for the fact that it was your own actions that angered the king in the first place (I'm not judging, just saying), it was an impressive escape. One of the office ladies suggested the problem was that the three of you hadn't taken a liking to the king's new statue. A word to the wise: the king is very keen on his statues, along with people bowing down to them, so I'd recommend you don't go angering him too often. Did you know he also keeps a den of lions who have a taste for human flesh? Surviving fire is one thing; surviving lions, well that's an entirely different matter.

On the day it happened, I saw the court magicians looking rather worried that they might be asked to replicate your escape. The last time I saw them, they were throwing their staffs on the ground in an attempt to turn them into ice cubes. I understand the furnace was heated seven times hotter than usual and the guards who threw you in were burnt to crisp before they could move away. Between you and me, I haven't come across anyone shedding tears for the guards. A friend standing fifty metres away said that even at that distance he could toast his marshmallows, and as he later discovered, he had toasted his eyebrows too. So then, it was a jolly hot furnace, and you three somehow survived it.

I'm sure you can appreciate that a certain level of curiosity and speculation has arisen as to how you were able to pull it off. If only you could have heard the gasps from the crowd when you walked back out alive. Not only alive, in fact, but without even a whiff of smoke on your clothes. Incidentally, I had a visit this morning from a Mr Nic O'Teen enquiring about those smoke-free clothes; he was interested in learning more. It has something to do with a new industry he's looking at establishing. He said smoke-proof clothes might stop wives asking their husbands questions about where they'd been the night before. None of it made any sense to me; perhaps one day in the future it might.

Clothing that could protect the wearer from fire could completely revolutionise the fire protection industry and save countless lives every year. Babylon Fire Safety Specialists Ltd. are extremely interested in discussing possible patent and trademark arrangements which could be mutually beneficial to both parties. Once proven and certified, the products could earn you a large sum of money.

I've been told that the king, along with several of his officials, observed a fourth person in the fire, yet no one saw this person exit the furnace. Palace officials plan to look for their bones once the furnace has cooled enough, but in the meantime, can any of you shed light on the mystery figure?

I look forward to talking further shortly.

Yours,

Nabopolasarr

DISCUSSION

THREE MEN AND A STATUE

What do three Jewish lads, a large statue, one angry king, and an extra hot furnace have in common? You can read all about it in Daniel chapter three. The three lads in question—Shadrach, Meshach, and Abednego—had been taken into exile, along with Daniel, from their home in Judah. They were given new names to force them to blend into Babylonian culture and remove their Jewish identity. Today we might call it a case of forced assimilation.

> *The chief official gave them new names:*
> *to Daniel, the name Belteshazzar; to*
> *Hananiah, Shadrach; to Mishael, Meshach;*
> *and to Azariah, Abednego.*
>
> *Daniel 1:7*

The ruler of Babylon, King Nebuchadnezzar, made a large gold statue of himself and was tricked into ordering everyone to bow down to it when the music played. It was musical chairs, but with the twist that all the action takes place when the music starts rather than when it stops. If you weren't observed worshipping the statue when the music started, you were thrown into a blazing furnace. What a jolly fun day out—tea and cucumber sandwiches anyone?

THE FOURTH MAN

In this story, God demonstrates both his power over a physical process (fire) and his protection over the righteous. The Bible declares God to be our ever-present help in times of trouble (Psalm 46:1), and Shadrach, Meshach, and Abednego—well, they were definitely in trouble and they definitely needed some help.

When our three brave lads refused to bow down to the statue, they were thrown into the furnace. Usually, this would have resulted in anguished screaming and . . . but wait, there were suddenly *four people walking around in the flames. Even King Nebuchadnezzar* noticed that three men had turned into four:

> He said, "Look! I see *four men walking around in the fire, unbound and unharmed, and the fourth looks like a son of the gods.*"
>
> Daniel 3:25

Most Bible commentators believe this fourth person to be Jesus, making an Old Testament appearance before showing up later in the New Testament. How does he do this? Well, it's easier than you might think. Despite claims of various groups to the contrary, Jesus wasn't created, but has eternally existed as part of the Godhead—Father, Son, and Holy Spirit. Therefore, making an appearance at this point in history before being born on earth in human form wouldn't have been a difficult thing for him to do. Such appearances of Jesus (and there are several scattered throughout the Old Testament) are referred to as *Christophanies* (worth twenty-four points in Scrabble without any double or triple bonus scoring).

Another possibility is that the fourth figure was an angel sent to comfort and reassure the three men they weren't going to burn to death (always nice to know when you're inside an extra hot furnace). Paul had a similar angelic pep-talk experience during a shipwreck (Acts 27:23-24).

NO MATTER THE OUTCOME

In times of stress or danger, many Christians have found great comfort in Psalm 91:

> If you say, "The Lord is my refuge," and you make the Most High your dwelling, no harm will overtake you, no disaster will come near your tent. For he will command his angels concerning you to guard you in all your ways; they will lift you up in their hands, so that you will not strike your foot against a stone . . .
>
> vv. 9-12

> "Because he loves me," says the Lord, "I will rescue him; I will protect him, for he acknowledges my name. He will call on me, and I will answer him; I will be with him in trouble, I will deliver him and honor him. With long life I will satisfy him and show him my salvation."
>
> vv. 14-16

That said, life comes with no guarantees, and one must balance having confidence in the provisions of Psalm 91 (or any other scripture)

with the approach taken by these three lads who were thrown into the fire. They were confident God *could* rescue them (which on this occasion he did), but they had already determined they would acknowledge him as God and refuse to worship King Nebuchadnezzar's statue, whatever the outcome.

> *"If we are thrown into the blazing furnace, the God we serve is able to deliver us from Your Majesty's hand. But even if he does not, we want you to know, Your Majesty, that we will not serve your gods or worship the image of gold you have set up."*
>
> *Daniel 3:17-18*

Many Christians suffering from terminal medical conditions take this approach: God may heal me, but if he doesn't, I'll still acknowledge and worship him as God. This sense of serving and acknowledging God regardless of life-or-death outcomes is affirmed in Romans 14:8.

> *If we live, we live for the Lord; and if we die, we die for the Lord. So, whether we live or die, we belong to the Lord.*

Shadrach, Meshach and Abednego faced death for refusing to abandon their God and worship a man-made idol. After all the drama was over, they not only lived but came out of it with a promotion (Daniel 3:30). No one chooses to find themselves in such situations but as Christians, we can trust that even if we should die, we still can't lose. A joyful eternity with Jesus awaits.

THE OLD MAN AND THE LIONS

Nabu Shukura
Administration Services
Office of Public Affairs

Izdubar
Public Executioner
Royal Housing Estates

Reign of King Darius the Mede

Dear Izdubar,

Recently, King Darius issued a decree requiring everyone in the kingdom to pray to the king for a period of thirty days—a most reasonable requirement indeed. Belteshazzar (aka Daniel, one of the exiles from Judah) refused to do so and continued praying to his own God. For disobeying the decree, he was sentenced to death—a most reasonable punishment indeed.

His execution was to have been conducted using the lions—you know, those hungry large-sized cats we keep on hand: Elsa, Tiddles, Sheba, Leo, and my personal favourites, the twins Fang and Claw. However, I've just found out the execution was *unsuccessful*. Daniel was thrown to the lions, and the lions apparently took the night off. I hear they didn't lay a paw on him, let alone eat one of his fingers, and the next morning he walked out into the sunshine without a single scratch.

How hard can it be, Izdubar, to motivate a pack of lions to kill and eat one old man, who I'm told is pushing eighty? I've checked the Public Executions Register, and never before has there been a failure involving the use of the lions. To put it another way, lions are always hungry. Do you have a pet cat, Izdubar? Cats, as all cat owners know, are always hungry. Their hunger returns about thirty seconds after you feed them. Lions are just bigger versions of pet cats, always ready to eat another human thirty seconds after they finish off the last one. So, what went wrong? Surely, they must have had room in their bellies to fit in one more troublesome Jewish exile?

As soon as Daniel was removed, others whom the king believed were guilty of a conspiracy against him were thrown in. Can you guess what happened? Yes, Izdubar, that's right, the lions devoured them immediately! Clearly, they were hungry after all—especially Fang! So why didn't they eat Daniel? One explanation for this failure is incompetency on your part, but there's another, more troubling, line of enquiry. You see, my dear Izdubar, I have discovered that when, as a young man, you held the position of Public Executioner, another execution ended in failure. This incident dates back to the rule of King Nebuchadnezzar and concerns a fire furnace and three young Jewish lads. Instead of dying in flames, the boys walked out alive.

This feat would have been impossible without help, and jolly well near impossible even with help. Help that perhaps you were providing, Izdubar? There was talk of a fourth man being involved. Was he your assistant, perhaps? Should it turn out that you had any involvement in their survival, that would be most unfortunate indeed. Not unfortunate for the lions of course, especially Fang and Claw.

A single failure involving the lion pit might be excusable. I'm almost willing to accept that a lion, even several, can have an 'off day'. But failures involving both the lions and the fire furnace—I'm not buying it, especially when both cases involve Jewish exiles. There's talk that you might be protecting these people, or that you may even have Jewish blood yourself. Do you? King Darius might have a soft spot for Daniel and believe his story that God sent his angel and shut the mouths of the lions,[22] but

22 Daniel 6:22. Although Daniel was also exiled to Babylon, it is unclear why we don't read about him alongside Shadrach, Meshach and Abednego for refusing to bow down to the gold statue. Holding a high government position, he may have been away at the time or exempt from having to do so. Nevertheless,

you and I know better.

I'm sure, Izdubar, that you have no desire to become lion food yourself, so consider this your final warning. We certainly wouldn't want stories spreading that these Jewish exiles can't be killed by lions or fire. Some might start to believe that the God they worship is more powerful than the gods we worship, and that could lead to all manner of complications. So, do your job properly, and all will be fine. You don't want your friends and relatives to read about you in the newspaper, do you? Think of the headlines: "Lions Execute Public Executioner" or "Man Who Fed Lions Fed To The Lions." If there is another failure, I might have to take up writing myself. I quite fancy the idea of a children's book with the title: *Fang and Claw Eat Izdubar for Lunch*.

Yours,

Nabu Shukura

---

he too eventually faced his own life-or-death loyalty test.

DISCUSSION

HISTORY OF THE EXILES

This story takes place when Daniel is living in exile from his Judean homeland. There were two main exiles: One was conducted by the Assyrian empire (approximately 721 B.C.), and a second was conducted over a hundred years later in several stages by the Babylonian empire.

The King of Assyria removed the ten tribes in the northern kingdom of Israel relocating them to Assyria (2 Kings 17:5-6) and replacing them with non-Jewish people from his own kingdom (2 Kings 17:24), whereas the Babylonians took people (including Daniel and his three friends) from the southern kingdom of Judah. These exiles ended up roughly 1500 kilometres away in Babylon (modern-day Iraq). Daniel was taken in the first wave of Babylonian deportations[23] around 605 B.C. A second (597 B.C.) and third (586 B.C.) wave followed—though the exact dates are still debated. After living in Babylon for seventy years, the exiles were allowed to return to Jerusalem to rebuild the broken city wall (see the Book of Ezra).

The Assyrian exiles were never sent back to their home. That said, during the reign of King Asa, many people belonging to various northern tribes migrated south before the exile began.

> *. . . for large numbers had come over to him from Israel when they saw that the Lord his God was with him.*
>
> 2 Chronicles 15:9

Those who relocated would have brought with them their tribal identity. For how long such identities were maintained remains unknown, and this has resulted in much speculation. Some speak of the 'ten lost tribes' of Israel, while others believe some level of independent identity continued and the ten tribes didn't completely vanish from history.

THE KINGS WHO RULED OVER DANIEL

Daniel arrived in Babylon as a teenager and ended up serving under four kings. The first three were King Nebuchadnezzar II (or Nebuchadnezzar the Great), King Belshazzar, and King Darius the Meade. In around 539 B.C., Cyrus, King of Persia, captured Babylon and took over its reign. By this point, Daniel may have been in his early nineties. It was Cyrus who issued the decree allowing for the exiles to return to Jerusalem (Ezra 1:1-4). Daniel, however, stayed on—perhaps because he was settled there and it would have been a major trip for an old man to make.

---

23 For more details on the Babylonian exile see 2 Kings 24.

A MESSAGE FOR THE EXILES

The prophet Jeremiah sent a letter to those taken into exile, telling them to settle down in Babylon and live life normally for the next seventy years, after which God would come and get them. Despite it not being their true home, they were to live as though it was—not to fade away, but to continue on and increase in numbers.

> Build houses and settle down; plant gardens and eat what they produce. Marry and have sons and daughters; find wives for your sons and give your daughters in marriage, so that they too may have sons and daughters. Increase in number there; do not decrease.
>
> Jeremiah 29:5-6

This advice didn't completely stop them from having bouts of homesickness, as recorded in Psalm 137:1-4:

> By the rivers of Babylon we sat and wept when we remembered Zion.
>
> v. 1

A QUESTION OF LOYALTY

Two of the major events from the book of Daniel—the fire furnace and lions' den—involve Jewish exiles being challenged in their loyalty to worship only the one true God. On both occasions, their loyalty risked their lives.

Today, choosing not to believe the same things or act as others do in a secular world can result in criticism, prejudice, or even social rejection.

Joseph of Arimathea was a disciple of Jesus, but in secret (John 19:38). Sometimes, a little secrecy may be called for. When Jesus sent out the twelve disciples, he cautioned them:

> "I am sending you out like sheep among wolves. Therefore be as shrewd as snakes and as innocent as doves."
>
> Matthew 10:16

A MARTYR FOR THE CAUSE

In the case of the furnace and the lions, God performed two miraculous rescues. Such rescues still happen today, as missionaries and many other believers can testify, but they don't always happen. Sometimes, people become martyrs for the Christian cause.

In the New Testament, John the Baptist, James and Stephen were all killed instead of being rescued. Why some people get to live while others die is something only God can explain. What we do know is that God says the death of even one of his saints in precious in his eyes (Psalm 116:15).

DARIUS WHO?

Darius was the king who sent the three young lads to the furnace and Daniel to the lions' den. Yet, there has been some debate as to who Darius was, and whether he even existed. Then again, there has even been debate amongst secular scholars about whether King David ever existed, due to so little archaeological evidence.[24]

A lack of archaeological evidence for a biblical figure is nothing new. Isn't it odd, though, how some will deny the existence of historical figures such as Darius and David because of a lack of archaeological evidence yet believe in the existence of a non-physical afterlife which has *no* such evidence to support it (although the empty tomb of Jesus could be viewed as archaelogical evidence).

There are several reasons that may explain the difficulty in matching Darius's name to an individual in the historical record. Many people become better known by a name other than their birth name. For example, most people do not know that the singer Cliff Richard was actually born Harry Webb. Sir Elton John started out as Reginald Kenneth Dwight, and Caryn Elaine Johnson is better known professionally as Whoopi Goldberg. Likewise, King Darius may not have been born 'Darius'.

Another explanation is that ancient rulers would sometimes become known by their title. Some have suggested the name 'Darius' actually describes a position (rather than being a person's name) equivalent to governor. Nevertheless, our focus should not be on the quantity of archaeological evidence for specific biblical figures but on God's provision, guidance, and interventions in the lives of those who served and worshipped him.

---

24 There may be little archaeological evidence for King David, but that's not to say there is none. There is the Tel Dan Stele which was discovered in several pieces in northern Israel between 1993-1994. See wikipedia.org/wiki/Tel_Dan_stele

THE PROPHET AND THE WHALE

Jonah
Prophet of God
Gath Hepher

Religious Employees Assistance Programme
Disputes and Grievances Department
Section B: Prophets and Priests

Date: 760 B.C.

Dear Sir,

I am a prophet who goes places on behalf of God to announce blessings, anoint new kings, and deliver messages. Sometimes messages involve telling people to repent, which is easier said than done as often people don't want to repent. They can be stubborn and instead want to throw you in jail or saw you in half. Anyway, I was getting along fine with my employer, tackling various tasks for him, until a recent job he wanted me to do changed everything.

God's instruction was to travel to Nineveh (capital of the Assyrian empire) and tell the Ninevites to repent. It was a bit weird really, God sending *me*—a Jewish prophet—to a non-Jewish nation. Anyway, religio-political factors aside, the whole thing just wasn't my scene, and as it so happened, I was due a holiday. As they say, "there's no time like the present."

Now, it's true that, at that very moment, Nineveh was 500 miles to the east and my holiday plans required me travelling 2500 miles to the west. Thus, once I'd crossed the

Mediterranean by boat to Tarshish in Spain I would be 3000 miles from Nineveh. The fact that I would end up that far from Nineveh was pure coincidence. If the Nineveh job was urgent, surely my employer could have found someone else to do it—an enthusiastic trainee from the school of the prophets[25] keen to make a name for himself, for example. He'd become famous overnight—if he lived.

My holiday started well enough, with sunshine, blue skies, and fresh ocean air filling my lungs. Unfortunately, however, my employer wanted me back at work immediately. Suddenly, giant waves threatened to tear the boat to pieces, and the crew went into full-on panic mode. They started praying, which was sort of good, but unfortunately, their prayers were directed towards an assortment of strange and foreign gods. When their prayers went unanswered they moved on to throwing cargo overboard. That didn't work either, and, after drawing straws, they became convinced *I* was the problem. Little old me.

I explained that my employer was the creator of heaven and earth, and that currently he and I were in a little disagreement over my work/life balance. I then suggested the weather conditions would improve if they threw *me* overboard, but foolishly they didn't listen and instead tried rowing back to shore. Wrong move! When they did eventually turf me into the sea, a large fish turned up at just the wrong moment and had me for lunch. Ever wondered what a fish looks like on the inside? Alas, it's not very exciting—dark, slimy, and smelly. And no, I have no idea what creature I was swallowed by. I'm a prophet, you know, not a marine biologist.

After quite some time, the smell and sloshing around was getting to me, so I changed my mind and told my employer I was willing to put my holiday on hold and take the Nineveh job after all. Suddenly, pitch blackness turned to daylight, and I was vomited out like an unpleasant clump of seaweed. I made myself look respectable and headed to Nineveh where I delivered the message—all eight words of it.[26] Since my employer has the final say on all matters, I don't get consulted. But you'd think that after all I'd been through—and it was a lot—I'd at least get to see lightning fall and wipe out a few

---

25 2 Kings 2:3 speaks of a 'school of the prophets' or 'company of the prophets'.

26 Jonah's warning message was: "Forty more days and Nineveh will be overthrown" (Jonah 3:4). Today Nineveh is known as Mosul (located in modern Iraq).

Ninevites. Instead, the heathens put on sackcloth, covered themselves in ashes, and repented. I don't think I've ever been so disappointed in my life.

That sort of mass repenting does nothing for my reputation as a prophet. Nothing! My employer is merciful and forgiving,[27] which means I regularly end up going places to warn of forthcoming judgement but never get to see it actually take place. Where's the fun in that? Where's my employer going to find another prophet who will put up with him being nice? Recently graduated prophets have grown up on stories of Elijah killing false prophets and lightning falling on soldiers. They want to see action and destruction, establish themselves a reputation, develop gravitas. It's hard to do any of those things if people keep repenting.

I'm hoping you can negotiate a settlement with my employer on my behalf that compensates me for embarrassment suffered, a ruined holiday, and loss of non-refundable deposits. In addition, I would appreciate compensation for my tarnished reputation and the nightmare of living inside a fish for three days. And don't get me started on what the experience has done to my mental health. At a minimum, I'll never be able to eat fish again—far too triggering. I'll probably struggle to even holiday within a mile of an ocean for the rest of my life.

Much aggrieved,

Jonah
Prophet of God

---

27 "I knew that you are a gracious and compassionate God, slow to anger and abounding in love, a God who relents from sending calamity" (Jonah 4:2).

DISCUSSION

THE LEGITIMACY OF JONAH'S STORY

The story of Jonah is an all-time Sunday School favourite starring a prophet on the run, silly sailors, a whopper of a whale, and some naughty Ninevites. There are even non-speaking parts for a plant, a worm, and as many Ninevites as one can fit on stage.

As the story involves Jonah being swallowed by a giant fish, some believe the events recounted can't possibly be real. Yet, the story was referred to twice by Jesus. Firstly, Jesus compared his upcoming entombment in the earth for three days and three nights with Jonah's time spent inside the fish (Matthew 12:40). Jesus again referred to Jonah (in Luke 11:30) as a sign to the Ninevites of their need to repent, just as he was a sign to this generation of their need to repent from their wicked behaviour.

LOCATION, LOCATION, LOCATION

The exact location of Tarshish where Jonah was headed remains uncertain, but it is thought by many to be on the Spanish coast, perhaps near modern-day Gibraltar. Nineveh was the capital city of Assyria, and it would likely have taken Jonah weeks to travel there by horse or camel. One lesson Jonah can teach us is that if we run away from what God wants us to be doing (or dealing with), he has ways of ensuring we circle back 'around the mountain' and more or less return to where we started from. We may not want to face or deal with an issue, but God may want us to—it's called Christian growth.

THE MYSTERY OF THE FISH

It is unclear exactly what swallowed Jonah. Some critics have pointed out that whales are not fish, therefore the Bible is wrong when it says a whale swallowed Jonah.

Today, the division between whales and fish is clearly understood, but that wasn't always the case, especially not several thousand years ago. It was only several hundred years ago that scientists began to classify the animal kingdom more seriously, and many of the life-form divisions we take for granted today didn't exist back then. Even if a Bible writer (or, more likely, a Bible translator) did get the description wrong, that by itself isn't evidence that the events never occurred. Critics also can't prove that it wasn't a whale.

The story of how God deals with his misbehaving prophet includes several supernatural elements. Thus, there may also be a supernatural aspect involved in relation to the creature that swallowed Jonah, including how he was kept alive inside the animal instead of drowning or being digested. When it comes to Jonah being 'vomited out', it's known that sperm whales vomit up 'ambergris'. This substance was once highly prized in perfume making but is now usually replaced with a synthetic equivalent.[28] Who ever thought whale vomit could smell so good?

FOCUS ON WHAT MATTERS

Ultimately, debates over word choice don't disprove an event happened, nor can they disprove God. Such debates only serve to distract from the larger issues the Bible focuses on—topics that include sin, forgiveness, sacrifice, purpose, and the afterlife.

---

28   A 9.5kg blob of ambergris was found inside a dead sperm whale that washed up on La Palma Island in the Canary Islands in July 2023. It was valued at around 500,000 Euros. www.theguardian.com/environment/2023/jul/04/las-palmas-pathologist-ambergris-block-dead-sperm-whale

LETTERS RELATING TO THE NEW TESTAMENT OF THE BIBLE

ZECHARIAH ALMOST BURNS HIS FINGER

Zechariah
Temple Serving Priest
Hill Country of Judea

Department of Priestly Administration (DPA)
Unit 15, Hezekiah Business Annex
Jerusalem

Date: 7 B.C.

PTSD Claim–Post Temple Service Disability

Dear Sir,

Please find attached a completed #TP-96 claim form relating to events I recently experienced while undertaking my official duties. At that time, the priestly division of Abijah was on the roster and I was chosen by lot to serve inside the temple. My responsibilities included displaying the shewbread and burning incense on the incense altar. As a regular priest, I work in the Holy Place section of the temple, which is separated from the Holy of Holies by a large curtain. That curtain is a true work of art. I dread the thought of anything ever happening to it.

I was attending to my duties when suddenly an angel appeared—only an arm's length away—just to the right of the incense altar. It was such a shock that I lost my concentration and almost burnt my finger. Fortunately, I didn't knock over the altar and set the curtain on fire—that would have been very bad indeed. The whole experience has left me with heart palpitations. Just so you're clear, angels appearing inside the temple is, to say the least, unusual. This one said his name was Gabriel,[29] and he'd come from the immediate presence of God. His claim was very believable, so I didn't doubt him. It's not for me to dictate how angels should go about their business, but a warning he was coming would have been nice.

In the second Chronicles scroll, there is an account of the dedication of the First Temple. On that occasion, the presence of the Lord appeared unexpectedly and was so strong that the priests couldn't stand to minister—or even stand up, so I've been told.[30] Knowing that history, one chooses not to rush their work, and besides, there's the curtain to think of. As Gabriel stood there, a shiver ran down my spine, my knees went weak (they aren't the strongest at the best of times), and my mouth turned dry. The experience scared me fresh out of shekels, and I'm not embarrassed to admit it.

As a result of our brief encounter, I can no longer speak—solid evidence of the trauma I experienced. Since I can no longer perform priestly duties such as singing and leading prayers, I'm currently at home recuperating. I think my wife has been affected by what happened to me too—she has recently been throwing up in the mornings, along with eating some really odd things. The other night she wanted freshly seared lamb chops covered in a pomegranate glaze. You'd have to be a Jerusalem MasterChef to cook that sort of food, and I'm just a humble priest. She was so insistent that I had to get hold of "Donkey Eats" to get it delivered. That donkey-delivered nosh is jolly expensive, especially on a priest's income. These strange food cravings must be due to the stress she suffered, don't you think? I'm not sure what else could possibly explain it.

Yours,

Zechariah

---

29 Gabriel (a messenger angel) and Michael (a warrior angel) are the only two angels mentioned by name in the New Testament. No scripture supports praying directly to an angel. They remain under God's direct control at all times.

30 2 Chronicles 5:14

DISCUSSION

FROM THE OLD TO THE NEW

The Old Testament closes with the book of Malachi and Jerusalem ruled by the Persians. The Greeks (led by Alexander the Great) take over around 332 B.C. and in 63 B.C. the Romans turn up to take charge and are still present when Zechariah enters the temple. This made a gap of around 400 years between Old and New Testaments.

GOD'S PROVIDENCE AT WORK

It was King David who divided the temple priests into a roster of twenty-four divisions (1 Chronicles 24:3), each serving at the temple twice a year. When Zechariah's Abijah division—number eight on the roster—arrived in Jerusalem for duty, he was drawn by lot (Luke 1:8-10) to enter the temple to perform the required priestly duties. His selection may have appeared random, yet God had foreordained it, just as he does today with some of our own seemingly 'random' encounters with others.

THE TEMPLE FURNISHINGS

The interior of Jerusalem's Temple comprised two main areas: the Holy Place and Holy of Holies, separated from one another by a large curtain. The Holy Place, where Zechariah ministered, was hall-like in appearance and housed three main items:

A lampstand (candlestick) made of solid gold (Exodus 25:31-40).

A wooden table covered with gold on which shewbread or 'bread of the presence' was placed weekly (Exodus 25:23-30).

The altar of incense (wood covered with gold) (Exodus 30:1-10).

The account involving Zechariah and the angel is the only one in the entire New Testament that takes place within the innermost part of the temple. The Chamber of Hewn Stone (the Sanhedrin council chamber) was part of the temple but not part of the interior section where priests undertook their duties. Even Jesus never entered this inner section of the temple.

In the First Temple (destroyed in the early sixth century B.C.) the Holy of Holies housed the Ark of the Covenant. However, by the time of the Second Temple (the one standing at the time of Jesus), the ark had been lost.[31]

---

31 Tradition holds that around the time of the Babylonian invasion of 586 B.C., the ark was lost. It appears God intended this to happen, at least according to Jeremiah 3:16. Some think God may have relocated the ark to heaven (Revelation 11:19). This heavenly ark may be the original, some other ark, or merely be symbolic of something else. If it is the original ark, it would explain why, despite thousand of years of searching, it has never been found on earth.

AN AWKWARD CONVERSATION

Imagine with me, a senior priest having an uncomfortable conversation with a junior priest.

"Let me get this straight, you've lost the Ark of the Covenant?"

"Correct."

"The national symbol of the Israelites, gone—just like that?"

"Ahh . . . yes, I'm afraid so."

"Care to explain how this may have happened?"

"Not really."

"Did you let the Philistines steal it?'"

"Certainly not."

"Does the High Priest know it's missing?"

"Not yet, I was sort of hoping you might tell him for me . . ."

AN ANGELIC ENCOUNTER

In the Holy Place, the angel Gabriel appears to Zechariah (Luke 1:11-13). He tells him God is going to answer his prayer regarding his wife Elizabeth having a baby—something she'd been unable to do—and that the child was to be named John. Zechariah has a bit of an argument with the angel about the possibility of his wife getting pregnant due to her old age (Luke 1:18-20). Doubting the angel was a bad move by Zechariah who, in actual fact, was expressing doubt in God, who had sent the angel. As a priest, he should have known

better; and as an old, experienced priest, he *definitely* should have known better.

THE SWEET SOUND OF SILENCE

God lets Zechariah off lightly—he is unable to speak for nine months until John is born. Nine glorious months of peace and quiet for his wife Elizabeth! One can imagine her conversations with the neighbours:

"Oh Elizabeth, you're so lucky, I wish my husband would shut up for nine months and not say anything. Remind me again how you got him to stop talking?"

"So, he hit his thumb with a hammer and said nothing—not a sound? Not a single naughty word passed his lips? Amazing!"

THE LIFE AND MINISTRY OF JOHN

John is born, and later heads into the desert to live, clothing himself in a camel-hair garment and eating honey and wild locusts (Matthew 3:4). Part of his ministry involved baptising people, which is why he's often called John the Baptist. However, his most important role was to announce the forthcoming arrival of Jesus. Unfortunately, John ended up in jail and was beheaded as the result of a rash oath uttered by Herod Agrippa I during his birthday party (Matthew 14:1-12).

When Jesus heard of John's death, he took time to be alone and grieve (Matthew 14:13). The mothers of John and Jesus (Elizabeth and Mary) were related, which meant Jesus and

John, born only months apart, were also related. Evidently, Jesus felt his loss deeply. Since Jesus suffered emotional and physical pain, loss, scorn, disappointment, betrayal, rejection and the like during his earthly ministry, he can uniquely identify with how we feel when we experience similar situations. Not only does Jesus identify with our earthly experiences, but he provides comfort, compassion, and hope to help mend our broken hearts.

UNEXPECTED PREGNANCY, SECRET DIVORCE

Joseph the Carpenter
Isaiah Lane, 7-14
Nazareth

Rubin, Geller & Weinberg
Family Lawyers
Nazareth Legal Precinct

Date: 6 B.C.

Dear Sir,

Re: Divorcing my wife (quietly)

You are said to be the most discreet lawyer in the land, and for my little problem I definitely need 'discreet'. Not long ago, I was busy in my workshop when a woman dropped in with her very attractive daughter, Mary. We shared an enchanted gaze across my sawdust-filled workshop. Not that my workshop is always full of sawdust, you understand—I sweep it clean each night. After all, the last thing I want is to be blown to pieces in a sawdust explosion. Anyway, a single glance is all it took for me to know Mary was the girl of my dreams, and we are now engaged.

My life was one big blue piece of sky until a dark storm cloud appeared, and I discovered Mary had eyes for someone else. It turns out she is pregnant! I know there are stories told behind the camel sheds at school that you can get pregnant by holding hands, but I know they aren't true. Besides, I've barely even held her hand. I was shocked, to say the least. My first thought was that the boy from Mount Carmel Bakery was the culprit. They say he's a bit of a ladies' man, and I've seen them talking together on one occasion. Mary says she's not interested in other men, but she's pregnant, so she must have been interested in someone—or at the very least, someone was interested in her. No other explanation is possible.

When I challenged her, she tried to convince me the pregnancy wasn't her doing. She said it was 'special' and 'different' to other pregnancies, and no man came near her. Do I have 'stupid' stamped on my forehead? Pregnancies don't happen without a man being involved, and that man certainly wasn't me. Naturally, I don't believe her—what sane individual would? I asked more questions, attempting to get to the bottom of the matter, but she's sticking firmly to her story. She even claims an angel had told her she was going to get pregnant—like I was going to believe that. Seeing I wasn't convinced, she tried claiming that God was somehow involved. I don't believe that either.

If those wild claims weren't enough, she performed an unexpected gender reveal by blurting out that the baby is going to be a boy, and we have to call him Jesus. The only thing blue was the colour I turned after going into shock and forgetting to breathe. She said he will grow up to do great things later in life—as though 'doing great things' would somehow make everything okay. Anyway, how does she know what the child's going to do? I was initially struck with what a well-behaved young Jewish woman she was. Then again, teenage pregnancy numbers have been soaring in recent years.

I could take her to the temple and explain what has happened, but to be honest, I can't stand the thought of a bloodthirsty pack of priests stoning her to death—even if the law does allow it. Therefore, I was hoping that you would be able to organise a quiet divorce settlement on my behalf. This way, she gets to live, and I can get on with my life again.

Yours,

Joseph

DISCUSSION

BOY MEETS GIRL

When we are first introduced to Joseph and Mary it's like arriving late for a movie and finding it's already started. How did they meet? Who are their parents? Did they grow up with siblings? The Bible remains silent on these and other details. We are told Mary was a virgin, however, and pledged to be married to a man named Joseph (Luke 1:27).

THE AGE-OLD QUESTION

Mary is told by an angel she is about to become pregnant by supernatural means (Luke 1:26-35). Recognising this as God's plan for her life, she accepts it, commits to it, and, in turn, shows a deep level of maturity and trust. Mary's age is not given in the biblical account, but neither is it recorded in any reliable non-biblical historical record. This had led many to speculate (without proof) that she was quite young, perhaps only twelve to fifteen years old.

In Mary's culture at that time, teenage marriages and pregnancies were common (as they were in many western countries until the 1950s and 1960s). Furthermore, she had already chosen to get married, so she could just have easily become pregnant by Joseph at a similar age. Nevertheless, Mary's age is not the key detail we should be focusing on. God knew Mary was physically and emotionally mature enough to deal with both pregnancy and childbirth. She also had the mental toughness to handle the additional challenges she and Joseph would face over the following few years.

A DELICATE PROBLEM

Jewish marriage at that time was markedly different to its modern-day western equivalent. Joseph and Mary's engagement was considered marriage 'part one' and breaking it off required getting a *divorce*. However, in the eyes of the law they still weren't considered fully married and weren't living together. Thus, for Mary to be engaged and pregnant would have been viewed as sinful. Soon after becoming pregnant, Mary travelled south to Judea (around 145 kilometres away) to visit her relative Elizabeth for three months (Luke 1:39-40).

Perhaps Mary told Joseph of the pregnancy when she came home, having first had time to talk things over with her older cousin. Or maybe, on meeting her upon her return, Joseph noticed she had either eaten far too much of Elizabeth's home cooking or had somehow got herself pregnant.[32] Under the circumstances, Joseph's plan to divorce Mary was reasonable.

---

32   Some have tried to claim Mary's virgin birth was a case of parthenogenesis. This is a biological process whereby some plants, insects and animals can produce offspring without involving sexual reproduction, relying instead on a type of asexual reproduction. However, when it comes to humans, two things apply: 1) Currently there is no record of a human birth resulting from pure parthenogenesis (see www.newscientist.com/article/mg14819982-300-the-boy-whose-blood-has-no-father) and 2) As women only carry the X chromosomes, and a Y chromosome is required to make

Despite the emotional pain and probable sense of betrayal he was feeling, the divorce option allowed him to spare her life and shield her from public shame.

Because Joseph her husband was faithful to the law, and yet did not want to expose her to public disgrace, he had in mind to divorce her quietly.

Matthew 1:19

Applying the Law (Leviticus 20:10) would have resulted in Mary being stoned to death for committing adultery. On the other hand, even a quiet divorce may have required disclosure of Mary's pregnancy, which still could have resulted in her being stoned. Either way, Mary risked ending up dead. So, what was the solution? Well, I see your Leviticus 20:10 (stone the adulteress) and raise you a Deuteronomy 24:1 (quiet divorce).

Although she was pregnant, Mary hadn't actually committed adultery, so technically Leviticus 20:10 didn't apply. Deuteronomy 24:1 allowed a man to divorce his wife for almost any reason just by giving her a certificate of divorce. Thus, using this method, Joseph could have quietly slipped her a divorce note and avoided the religious courts.

If a man marries a woman who becomes displeasing to him because he finds something indecent about her, and he writes her a certificate of divorce, gives it to her and sends her from his house . . .
(Deuteronomy 24:1)

A JOB WELL DONE

Since Mary's pregnancy was the result of a supernatural event, Joseph had no way of knowing it wasn't the result of the usual 'boy meets girl'. So, God sent an angel to him in a dream (Matthew 1:21-25) to explain what was happening. He was told that taking a pregnant Mary into his house as his wife (thus completing 'part two' of the marriage contract) was the morally right thing to do.

Joseph subsequently raises a child who is not biologically his own, remains committed to his wife, and protects her reputation. Although young and newly married, he forgoes marital relations[33] until after Jesus is born (Matthew 1:25). Well done, Joseph, I salute you, sir! Well done to Mary also, rising to the challenge of having the course of her life unexpectedly altered.

---

a biological male, an unassisted human pregnancy of a male child by parthenogenesis is not possible. Therefore, the birth of Jesus required divine intervention.

33 The Catholic Church teaches that Joseph and Mary never had intimate relations and Mary remained a virgin forever (perpetual virginity). This teaching, together with the Immaculate Conception and Assumption of Mary, is rejected by the Protestant church, as there are no biblical scriptures to support such ideas.

A MATTER OF TRUST

Why does God allow us to face and wrestle with difficult situations even when they will ultimately work out fine in the end? One reason may be that walking through the difficulty itself reveals our heart. How did we respond? Could we have done it differently or better? How much did we trust God in the midst of the situation? Did we seek his help early in the process or did we hold out as long as we could, trying to deal with it ourselves? Did we trust him more than the last time things got difficult? Only by walking through difficulties will the true mettle of our faith be tested.

STILL PREGNANT BUT NO DIVORCE

Joseph the Carpenter
Isaiah Lane, 7-14
Nazareth

Rubin, Geller & Weinberg
Family Lawyers
Nazareth Legal Precinct

Date: 6 B.C.

Re: Not divorcing my wife

Dear Sir,

I wrote to you recently to ask for your assistance in quietly divorcing the young woman to whom I am engaged. However, I no longer wish to proceed with this. When I last wrote, I suggested she had tried muddying the waters regarding the circumstances of her pregnancy by turning the situation into a religious one. People do that sometimes by claiming, "God told me so," or in Mary's case, "an angel told me so," when in reality it usually isn't true.

I'm sure you know how it goes. Boy sees an attractive girl and takes a liking to her. Then, a little later, in a heightened emotional state, he comes across a pile of leaves. In his eyes, the pile of leaves takes on the shape of a heart, and he interprets that as a sign from God, convincing him he should marry her. The next thing you know, he's telling everyone who will listen that God spoke to him through a pile of leaves and told him he was to marry the girl. The girl, meanwhile, knows nothing about the situation and hasn't even met the boy. It would be different if the girl was seeing her own heart-shaped piles of leaves. But, let's be honest, how often does that happen—especially when it's not autumn and the girl doesn't go walking?

When Mary said *God* told her she was going to get pregnant, what was I supposed to do? I could have said she was mistaken, but what if God really did tell her such a thing? I'd look pretty stupid arguing with God, wouldn't I? It's all a bit confusing really—her pregnancy has got a touch of the mysterious about it. Have you ever found yourself awake at 3 a.m., thoughts spinning in your head, pondering the mysteries of life? No? Then how about at 4 a.m? I see. You're a deep sleeper then, lucky you.

My letter suggested a boy from Mount Carmel Bakery may have been out and about sowing his wild oats. The reality is, however, he was far more likely to be at work, cooking them. Forget I mentioned him; it was a mistake on my part. It could have happened to anyone—probably not the High Priest, admittedly—but almost anyone else. Oh, and probably not King Herod either—but almost anyone apart from those two. The fact is, at the time, I wasn't fully informed about Mary's situation and made some rash assumptions. It won't happen again, I promise.

I'm sure you can appreciate this is a very delicate matter. Although I'm not the father, Mary hasn't done anything morally wrong. I think the word we are both searching for is . . . paradox. The thing is, these are unusual times in which we live—remember that old priest who got his equally-old wife pregnant? Was that unusual, or what? She had never been pregnant in her life, then suddenly a baby is on the way in her old age. Yet instead of running around telling everyone the good news, the husband remains absolutely silent. Just plain weird.

Anyway, not long after last writing to you, I collected Mary from her family home and took her back to my place. We are now fully married under the law, and I can assure you I have no desire or intention of divorcing her.

Yours, happily married,

Joseph (The Carpenter)

DISCUSSION

JOSEPH'S DREAM

Joseph faced a difficult decision: divorce his wife, who appeared to have committed adultery, or overlook her unfaithfulness and stay with her. We aren't told of any conversations the couple may have had, nor whether other people, such as her parents, knew about the pregnancy. Mary may have tried to explain to Joseph the supernatural aspect of the pregnancy, but, if so, it appears he remained unconvinced and still intended to divorce her. Instead, prompted by a dream in which God put Joseph's mind at rest, he took Mary home as his wife (Matthew 1:24-25). I can imagine his mind being a jumble of thoughts that night:

What's going on Lord? Why has all this happened? What does it all mean? I'm just a carpenter and now I'm being dragged into something written about in the ancient religious scrolls. I think I'll get up and make myself a hot drink—and maybe have a little cry. I'm just a carpenter—Zechariah's the religious one in the family. Isn't it enough that he's a priest and full-time religious worker? I'm told he argued with an angel, is that true? Why do you need me and Mary to be part of things, too? Couldn't I have just made a piece of furniture for the temple instead, then called it quits? This baby business isn't going to involve anything dangerous is it—like people trying to kill us? Or the baby? And no strangers please. Mary doesn't do strangers—especially not the kind who might turn up when she's got a new baby. I might be able to cope a little better if we got to go to Egypt. I've always wanted to see the pyramids. Could you perhaps fit Egypt into the plans?

BEING RECEPTIVE (AND OBEDIENT) TO GOD'S GUIDANCE

Stepping back slightly, we can see how God was bringing his plan to fruition—a plan that first originated in the Book of Genesis (Genesis 3:15). Long ago, God had promised mankind a deliverer, and with Mary's pregnancy, the arrival of that deliverer was only months away. That said, Jesus wouldn't begin his public ministry for another thirty years. Through no fault of his own, Joseph was about to upset that plan, so God stepped in to keep it on track. Fortunately, Joseph must have had a close enough relationship with God to understand the guidance he was being given in the dream, and he had the courage to act on it. Someone else may have acted differently.

God's guidance in our lives can come in a variety of different ways including a 'coincidence', a verse we read in the Bible, the involvement of angels (not that we would usually be aware of them), or through dreams and visions. On other occasions, someone may speak a prophetic word to us or quote a specific scripture.

THE CHRISTMAS STORY

Joseph the Carpenter
Isaiah Lane, 7-14
Nazareth

The Relatives
Date Palm Road
Bethlehem

Date: Jan 5 B.C.

Dear Relatives,

How's life in bustling Bethlehem these days? Has everyone recovered from the last Passover stampede? Sorry I haven't been to visit. Life up this way has been rather busy of late. However, I will be heading your way soon to register for the census Caesar Augustus ordered. Why I can't just fill out a form here in Nazareth and post it off beats me, but that's Roman bureaucracy for you. Anyway, I'll need—that is, Mary and I will need—somewhere to stay, and I thought to myself: *Who do I know who lives in Bethlehem?*

If we can stay with you, you'll all get to meet Mary. She's lovely. Did I mention she's having a baby and that we're married now? Perhaps I should have written that the other way around: married and baby on the way. I was sure I'd written and told you already, but perhaps not. Things got a little stressful when she announced her pregnancy. There's nothing to worry about—there was just a slight misunderstanding on my part, but it's all sorted now. I didn't misunderstand that she was pregnant, goodness no. I can recognise a pregnancy when I see one—that's what started the misunderstanding. You see, when she told me that . . . never mind.

I was hoping we could stay for a couple of months while we register for the census and have the baby. That way, once Mary's days of purification are over, we would both go to the temple for the child's dedication. Staying at your place would also allow us to catch an express cart into Jerusalem to pick up a few items we can't buy locally. Mary wants one of those new baby-higher-up chair things that have just come out. *Why don't I make one myself?* I hear you ask. Well, I would, but Mary wants a 'proper' one! There's nothing not proper about my woodwork, you understand, she's just being fussy. After sorting things at the temple, we'd be out of your way and headed home.

Our only alternative is to come to Bethlehem for the census, then return to Nazareth to have the baby—and hopefully make it in time (Mary would never forgive me if she had to have a roadside birth). Then, we would have to come back a few weeks later for the baby's dedication at the temple before returning home again. Obviously, there's a lot of extra travel and expense involved in doing it that way. We can't afford to stay in a local inn for that amount of time, and besides, who would want to? Have you ever looked up Bethlehem inns in the *National Inn Guide*? Most only get a one-star rating. Mary said our baby isn't going to have anything to do with only one star! I do love her, but she's been saying some really weird stuff lately.

I know it's a big ask, but it's not like a group of singing shepherds would unexpectedly turn up or anything else unusual. Speaking of visits, you could contact Zechariah and Elizabeth. I hear that after Elizabeth gave birth to baby John about six months ago, Zechariah started talking again (finally). They might be up to travelling by now, and if they were able to come, we could have a big family catch-up and dinner. It would be like—I can't quite think of the word I want—maybe Chris . . . Anyway, think it over, and let us know if it suits. I know Mary would be grateful. I did mention we are now married, didn't I?

Yours,

Joseph and Mary

DISCUSSION

A DRAMA-FILLED FIRST CHRISTMAS

The events of what we now call "the Christmas story" cover a possible timespan of up to two years. We jump in at the point where Joseph needs to take a family trip from Nazareth to Bethlehem to register for a census (Luke 2:1-3). What follows is something of a kerfuffle with accommodation[34] and birthing arrangements, shepherds turning up unexpectedly (Luke 2:15-17), and an encounter at the temple with a prophetess and an old man (Luke 2:27-38). Into the mix, we can add mysterious travellers from a faraway land bringing gifts for baby Jesus (Matthew 2:7-11). Also, don't forget about King Herod throwing a tantrum any two-year-old would be proud of, before ordering the death of all the baby boys aged two and younger (Matthew 2:16).

A MATTER OF TIMING

It is worth keeping in mind that, despite appearances, the recorded events in the Christmas story don't always follow in sequential order. This is especially true when it gets to the parts concerning the shepherds, the wise men, King Herod, and the escape to Egypt. There have been debates regarding Joseph and Mary's location at specific times, and some events—which take just moments to read—realistically would have played out over days or weeks.

EN ROUTE TO EGYPT

While in Bethlehem, Joseph is warned in a dream by God of Herod's intentions. He subsequently packs up their belongings and undertakes a nighttime evacuation of the family to Egypt (Matthew 2:13-15). At least he didn't have to worry about organising passports and visas. It is unclear how long they lived in Egypt, though estimates range from months to several years. As the couple pack, we may have heard the following conversation . . .

"Joseph, have you seen my brown sandals?"

"Which brown sandals? You've got three pairs."

"The dark brown ones I bought after we went to the temple."

"You bought new sandals? Does that make four pairs? Mary, you said you'd ask me first before buying new footwear."

"I didn't have time! They were the last pair in stock, and they were on special. Have you packed the gold Jesus was given?"

---

34 Many Bible scholars think Joseph and Mary were accommodated in a house, probably with relatives. The traditional nativity play narrative where Joseph and Mary—almost at the point of birth—arrive (often at night) to find there is 'no spare room in the inn' is difficult to support from the original Greek text. The Bible offers no sense of urgency regarding their arrival, and, at that time, bandits made travelling at night particularly dangerous. Instead, the text suggests that sometime after they arrived, Mary went into labour i.e., they arrived, settled in, and then the baby was born (Luke 2:6).

"Jesus got given some gold?"

"Stop being stupid! Have you found my sandals or not?"

"I've found the gold. Gosh, it's shiny, isn't it?"

"Sandals!!!"

"I'm looking, I'm looking . . ."

THE MYSTERIOUS MAGI

And then there are the Three Wise Men (Matthew 2:1-13)—or were there? The Bible only mentions three gifts, not three men. Were they gentiles, as clues in the text suggest? Did they travel with a military escort? How long did their journey take? Travelling from another country would have taken months, and they would have needed provisions, so perhaps there were three men and ten camels carrying supplies. How did they know the star they saw (Matthew 2:2) meant an extra special king was being born? Somehow, they knew the timing of Jesus's birth even though the Jewish leaders themselves didn't. Yet, they didn't know the exact location, but the Jewish leaders did (Micah 5:2).

Was the journey a private venture by individual wise men or an official foreign delegation? What convinced them in the first place that taking a journey to an unknown destination was worth risking their lives for? Did the star remain visible for their entire journey or appear, vanish, and reappear as required? What even was the 'star'? Was it a comet, a planetary conjunction (Jupiter and Saturn as some have suggested),[35] or a supernova? Perhaps it was simply God summoning into existence ball lightning?

Upon meeting baby Jesus, the wise men bowed down and worshipped him, giving us an early clue that Jesus would be a king for both Jews and gentiles. There has been speculation over the significance of the gifts they gave—gold, frankincense, and myrrh—yet all were considered valuable at the time.

Despite the passing of several thousand years, when it comes to the story of the *magi* ('wise men' in English), many mysteries remain. How did Matthew and Luke originally come to hear of the story and the associated events? Did some of the disciples hear Jesus talk about it over dinner one evening, or had it been written down somewhere? Mystery upon mystery remains. Yet, interesting as it may be to speculate, let us not get sidetracked from the main event: Jesus entering humanity for the first time in the form of a baby.

---

35 www.astronomy.com/science/the-star-of-bethlehem-can-science-explain-what-it-really-was/

WHO DID YOU SAY WE ARE RELATED TO?

Mordechai Rafa
Genealogy House
Jerusalem

Mary, wife of Joseph
Date Palm Road
Bethlehem

Date: Jan 5 B.C.

Dear Mary,

It was lovely of you to take some time out of your busy schedule to visit our office here in the city. I've been told that, as a result of some things spoken to you at the temple about your new son, Jesus, you've become interested in his genealogy. Listed below are some of his more notable relatives, but please be aware that this may make for uncomfortable reading.

Significant female ancestors

Tamar: Judah (one of Jacob's twelve sons) married and had three sons—one of which was Er.[36] Er married Tamar, but Er was so bad the Lord put him to death.[37] Er's brother Onan was supposed to carry on the family line with Tamar, but he wouldn't, so he too was put to death. I'll spare you the details, but Tamar resorted to dressing up as

---

36 Genesis 38:3
37 Genesis 38:7

77

a shrine prostitute[38] in order to get pregnant by her father-in-law. The end result was twins. One of the boys was named Perez, and six generations down the Perez line we arrive at Boaz.

Rahab: A Canaanite prostitute running a brothel (possibly called "The Naughty Nook") located inside the wall of Jericho city who provided accommodation for several Israelite spies before her city was captured and destroyed. She married Salmon from the tribe of Judah and became the mother of Boaz. It is very prestigious belonging to the tribe of Judah, even if it does require adding a prostitute into the family line to pull it off.

Ruth: Initially a Moabite widow. As you may have heard, the Moabite people have somewhat dark origins. It all dates back to when Lot and his family escaped the city of Sodom before its fiery destruction. As they escaped, Lot's wife—although warned against it—turned back (for one last look at her flower garden, perhaps?) and *wham* . . . she was turned into a pillar of salt.[39] Fortunately, Lot's two daughters both made it out alive, but their fiancés wouldn't follow and got turned to ash. The daughters then did the old Tamar trick. They got their father drunk and got themselves pregnant by him—the older daughter later giving birth to Moab, the father of the Moabites.[40] Anyway, Ruth went on to marry Boaz[41] and became the great-grandmother of King David.

Bathsheba: One evening King David spotted the rather beautiful Bathsheba from his rooftop and 'invited' her over to the palace. (She was married to a Hittite, making her a Hittite by marriage.) I'd like to say the visit was only for tea and scones, or roasting marshmallows fireside, but instead, there was some hanky-panky, which may or may not have been consensual.[42]

The king received a note saying she was pregnant but didn't repent from his sin. Instead, he organised for her husband to return home from the battlefield, hoping he'd engage

---

38 Genesis 38:13-19

39 Genesis 19:26 Note: The Bible doesn't make any mention of her looking at a flower garden.

40 Genesis 19:30-36

41 Ruth 4:13

42 2 Samuel 11:3-4 There has been debate surrounding how consensual their encounter was. When Nathan the prophet exposed what happened (2 Samuel 12:1-18), *all* the judgements fell on King David, suggesting Bathsheba had been a less than willing participant.

in some R&R with his wife and make it look like *he* was the father of the baby. This arrangement didn't go as planned, however, and David had Uriah killed in battle instead. Later, Nathan the prophet turned up and exposed David's sin in the matter. As punishment, David and Bathsheba's child died. Bathsheba's next pregnancy produced Solomon, who succeeded David as king.

Significant male ancestors

King David: Said to be a man after God's own heart.[43] Apart from the incident with Bathsheba, where David allowed his attention to focus on the creation and not on the Creator, he was also responsible for a census violation. This involved determining the size and strength of the army when he shouldn't have—a little error which cost 70,000 people their lives.[44] A lesser-known fact about King David is that he set up a music team of 288 people to minister before the Lord.[45]

Solomon: Organised the building of the First Temple and is said to be the wisest man who ever lived. He even impressed the Queen of Sheba who came to visit, answering even her hardest questions.[46] Now, I'm not one to spread gossip, but even today there are stories doing the rounds that suggest the Queen . . . ahem, let's just say after her visit she may have left pregnant, and Solomon may have been involved. It's probably just royal palace tittle-tattle. That said, Solomon was known to have had an eye for the ladies (somewhat like his father), amassing 700 royal wives and 300 concubines.[47]

Unfortunately, Solomon chose some wives who led him into worshipping foreign gods—something the Deuteronomy scroll said might happen.[48] It seems Solomon also had

---

43 1 Samuel 13:14; Acts 13:22

44 2 Samuel 24:9-15

45 1 Chronicles 25:7-8

46 1 Kings 10:1 The location of Sheba remains uncertain. Suggestions include the Kingdom of Axum in Ethiopia or the Kingdom of Saba in Yemen. Note: Ethiopia's modern borders differ to those of Ethiopia in the Bible.

47 1 Kings 11:3 Solomon had a son Rehoboam whose mother was Naamah, an Ammonite. This added Ammonite blood into the family line (1 Kings 14:21, Matthew 1:7).

48 Kings were prohibited from accumulating many wives (Deuteronomy 17:17).

a bit of a zoological interest and was known to import apes and baboons.[49] He either saw himself as a zookeeper or a fast food mogul, and the staff in the royal household were able to grab themselves a 'Big Baboon Burger'—but only for a limited time.

Rehoboam: a son of Solomon who married 78 women (2 Chronicles 11:21). Solomon's tax policies weren't too popular, but when Rehoboam became king and the ten northern tribes asked for tax relief, he refused. As a result of his heavy-handed threats, the northern tribes revolted, and the united kingdom of Israel split into two. Rehoboam remained king of the southern kingdom named Judah, and the ten rebelling tribes established a new northern kingdom called Israel. If splitting the kingdom wasn't bad enough, his next move could have been catastrophic. Upset about the northern tribes going their own way, Rehoboam assembled an army of 180,000 fighting men with the intention of 'sorting things out'. Fortunately for all involved, a bloodbath was prevented by the prophet Shemaiah.[50]

King Ahaz: the twelfth king of Judah. He became king at the age of twenty, and during the next two decades, he accumulated one of the greatest piles of evil deeds of any king before him or since. (Except for King Ahab, who really knew how to pile up the evil.) King Ahaz's evil deeds included making idols, making sacrifices in the high places, setting up altars to foreign gods, and committing sacrilege against the Lord's temple. He even had his own children burned alive as human sacrifices.[51] He shut the doors of the Temple of the Lord and set up altars to foreign gods on street corners! It was no surprise, then, that he wasn't buried with the other kings of Israel.[52]

Amongst your son's relatives are people responsible for major acts of sin that include adultery, incest, worshipping and making altars to foreign gods, dividing a nation, murder, drunkenness, sacrificing one's own children by fire, prostitution . . . It's really quite the list of moral shortcomings. You also have foreigners of the Canaanite, Hittite and Moabite variety, as well as a touch of Ammonite blood from Rehoboam's mother.

---

49 2 Chronicles 9:21

50 1 Kings 12:21–24

51 2 Kings 16:3

52 2 Chronicles 28:27

Fortunately, the evil deeds of one's ancestors don't prevent the later generations from achieving great things. I wish your new son well, and may the positive things spoken about him in the temple that day come to pass.

Yours,

Mordechai Rafa
Senior Genealogist

DISCUSSION

FAMILY DYSFUNCTION AT ITS FINEST

Jesus's family tree was about as messy as it gets; certainly there were enough morally questionable goings-on to bring shame on the family name. Yet, if you go back far enough in any family, something or someone unpleasant will almost always pop out of the woodwork—occasionally even an ardent Nazi from World War II.

In May 2012, the BBC published an article about Rainer Hoess[53] whose grandfather was Rudolf Hoess (not to be confused with the Nazi Party deputy leader Rudolf *Hess*). Rudolf, as it turned out, was the first commandant of the Auschwitz concentration camp where an estimated one million Jews were exterminated. On discovering this family history, Rainer commented:

> "It's hard to explain the guilt. Even though there is no reason I should bear any guilt, I still bear it. *I carry the guilt with me in my mind.*"

In 1997, Zygora Fank, a 62-year-old Jewish woman (accompanied by a television documentary team) travelled to Southern Poland to investigate property her grandfather was said to have owned before WWII. On it, he had operated a tar paper factory. Seized by the Germans, it eventually became part of the land on which Auschwitz (also known as Auschwitz-Birkenau) was built. It was converted into a munitions factory and operated using female slave labour from the Auschwitz camps.

Zygora discovered that her grandfather's property had been reclaimed after the war by her mother. Thus, by inheritance, Zygora had become the owner of land linked to the Auschwitz extermination camp, land on which most members of her mother's family had been killed. Her response?

> "This camp was built on Jewish land, and on the same land in the same camp, my whole family was gassed and shot and burned. *I don't have to feel guilty but I do.*"[54]

Even organisations can share a sense of guilt or shame over events or situations they aren't responsible for. This includes the Mount Hutt ski field located in the South Island of New Zealand. The Mount Hutt ski field was established by a number of people, including an immigrant by the name of Willi Huber. When Huber immigrated to New Zealand in 1953, he was known to have been a member of the Austrian army, as had thousands of his countrymen. In the 1970s, Huber assisted in establishing

53 www.bbc.com/news/magazine-18120890

54 www.nytimes.com/1998/07/10/world/hadera-journal-jewish-family-heirloom-15-square-miles-of-death.html

the ski field, and as a way of recognising his contribution to the community, one of its ski runs and food outlets carried his name. However, in 2021, details of his involvement with the Nazi Waffen-SS (very different to the regular German army) were exposed in a *North & South* magazine article.[55] There was significant public backlash, and as a result, the ski-run and food outlet were renamed.

FREEDOM FROM GENERATIONAL SHAME

Shame and guilt are powerful forces, and many people live with the shame of what others have done. And while few of us are likely to have a relative like Rudolf Hoess or become owners of land associated with an atrocity, every family has parts of their history they wish had not happened. Perhaps your story or family history includes a sexual scandal or two, adultery, incest, or someone getting pregnant to someone they shouldn't have. Maybe a family member deals drugs, has committed murder, or has sexually assaulted someone. Or perhaps a relative was deported from a country or joined up on the 'wrong' side of an armed conflict. Perhaps *you* are the child that resulted from someone else's 'David and Bathsheba' liaison or learnt your mother or father isn't the biological parent you always thought they were.

Jesus can free us from not only personal shame, but also the shame that others in our family might bring on us. On the cross, Jesus took not only our personal sin and shame but also the generational shame in our family.

A NEW FAMILY AWAITS

There's an old saying: "You can choose your friends, but you can't choose your relatives." How true that is. Jesus is fully aware of our checkered past and colourful family history yet still invites us to join his family.

Jesus knew exactly what he was getting when he died for us on the cross. God isn't put off by our shame and actions. We don't need to hold back from a relationship with him. Some people think they will never be accepted by God because of the terrible things they have done. But in Christ, our shame is taken away. Jesus already knows everything we have already done—none of our sin will ever surprise him! He's not put off by us! He does not disown us because of the sins or failures we have experienced. Other people may reel away in horror, but Jesus stands with his arms wide open.

Both the one who makes people holy and those who are made holy are of the same family. So Jesus is not ashamed to call them brothers and sisters.

Hebrews 2:11

While we were still sinners, Christ died for us.

Romans 5:8

---

55 *North and South.* June 2021 ed. www.northandsouth.co.nz/2021/06/17/willi-huber-mt-hutt-nazi/

God sees the real 'us'—warts and all—and he invites us into relationship, regardless of who may have snuck into the family gene pool when the lifeguard wasn't watching.

A LITTLE WHINE BRINGS
A LOT OF WINE

Jerusalem Wine & Beverage Co.

King Herod Boulevard

Jerusalem

Jesus the Carpenter

C/- Mary's House

Nazareth

Date: A.D. 27

Dear Jesus,

Last weekend, I attended a wedding in Cana and I saw you were there too. I had to laugh at the groom's speech when he said the night before the wedding he'd slept like a baby—waking up crying every two hours. I guess he was a little nervous!

Anyway, someone said you were a carpenter, but what I don't get is why a carpenter needs a group of twelve assistants? Handy, I suppose, if you need some heavy beams lifted into place or you're planning on building something large. Please tell me you aren't planning on building an ark as things got very wet around here the last time that happened, and the population dropped overnight—precariously so. Someone else suggested that you might be about to give up carpentry to follow a religious path in life, but that doesn't seem likely.

Speaking of religious things, it's been fairly quiet in that department around these parts, except of course for that strange occurrence about thirty years back. Some old priest went into the temple, and after being inside for about as long as one has to wait for a bank teller—assuming you can actually find a bank in the first place—he couldn't talk when he came out. It really makes you wonder what goes on inside the place. I keep hearing about some fancy curtain they've got. You don't suppose he might have accidentally set the thing on fire, do you? There's also another story concerning a young unmarried girl who got pregnant but insisted she was still a virgin. Pregnant and virgin, that made me laugh—they're definitely not two words that appeared in the same sentence where I went to school. Fortunately for the girl, some chap called Joseph swooped in, married her, and saved the day. How she escaped being stoned, I'll never know. Clearly, the law isn't being enforced like it used to be, and if God were to turn up, I bet he'd make a few changes. "Leave no stone un-thrown" is my motto, along with, "The only good bottle of wine is an empty one."

As it so happens, wine is the reason I'm writing. I saw you at that wedding, and what do you know, the wine ran out. The word on the street is that it was another botch-up by Job and Co. Wines. I didn't catch all the details, but I believe that when the great drink shortage struck, you stepped in to help, and almost instantly organised a considerable quantity of what is undoubtedly the best wine I've ever tasted. Even the wedding sommelier was impressed, and let me assure you, he's a man who has drunk an amphora or ten of the stuff. You're certainly onto a winner with that brew. With your excellent wine-making skills, and my extensive marketing and distribution networks, I know I can make you very successful in the wine business, and wealthy too.

Your share of the profits could be used to help fund your next venture—I'm sure it's not cheap feeding ex-fishermen. I bet those big boys have appetites the size of lions. Anyway, I was wondering if you have a name for your wine? Something that good could be called "King's Private Bin," or "King's Reserve." Let's get together soon, with a bottle or two of that stuff from the wedding, and we can discuss your promising future in the world of wine. What could be more important than that?

Yours,

Simeon
Wine Merchant Extraordinaire

DISCUSSION

JESUS'S FIRST MIRACLE

The story of Jesus turning water into wine at the wedding in Cana is well known and is considered his first public miracle. In those times, a Jewish wedding celebration could last for up to a week, just as some Indian wedding celebrations do today. Keeping the drinks flowing for an event lasting this long was undoubtedly a challenge, but why the wine ran out remains unknown. Perhaps more guests arrived than expected.

Running out of wine would be indicative of either careless planning or financial problems, both of which would have reflected poorly on the host family. When the wine ran out, Mary was not concerned for herself but for the reputation of the family whose event it was. She may have felt some responsibility for the situation or perhaps was involved with the wedding in some way. In her moment of need, Mary turned to Jesus for help, just as we are encouraged to seek God when we are in need. The Bible doesn't provide us with any real clues regarding her choice of action, but it's likely she either knew or felt strongly that Jesus would be able to help in some way.

After telling Jesus there's a problem with the drinks, she more or less immediately gives this instruction to the wedding's waiters: "Do whatever he tells you" (John 2:5). The wine is gone, the servants are waiting, and Jesus's mother has spoken in such a way that there is now an expectancy that something will happen. No pressure, Jesus, but there's a lot of people standing around with empty goblets all looking in your direction! Jesus comes to the rescue by turning a large quantity of water into an equal quantity of first-class wine (John 2:1-11). This water-to-wine miracle marked the start of Jesus's public ministry at the age of thirty—a ministry that is estimated to have lasted three to three-and-a-half years (Luke 3:23).

A SYMBOL OF GOD'S ABUNDANCE

The wine produced would roughly fill 900 x 750ml-sized bottles,[56] enough to open a small wine shop or stock a decent-sized cellar. This quantity of wine may appear excessive, but we aren't told how many more days of the celebration remained nor the total number of guests in attendance. Jesus may also have intended for some to be left over as a gift to the bride and groom. It would be contradictory for the Old Testament to issue warnings concerning the overconsumption of wine only for Jesus to come along and create enough for everyone present to get roaring drunk. These matters aside, the quantity of wine can be

---

56 John 2:6 states there were six jars, each holding twenty or thirty gallons. (20+30)/2 = 25 gallons average capacity per jar. 6x25 = 150 gallons total. 1 gallon (imperial) is 4.54 litres. 150 (gallons) x 4.54 litres = 681 litres. A standard wine bottle is 750ml (0.75 litres) 681/0.75L = 908 bottles.

seen as a reflection of the abundance found in the kingdom of God, something Jesus would spend the next few years preaching about.

Jesus would go on to give further demonstrations of abundance, including the feeding of more than five thousand people with nothing more than a boy's packed lunch of bread and fish.[57] Fish also featured in an abundant catch by Peter and his brothers. In this story we see how God is able to work with what we have, even if it is only our obedience (Luke 5:4-7). Sometimes, when we try and do things our own way or in our own strength, they don't work out. God may then get us to repeat the action with his support, and when that happens, the outcome can be quite different.

The fact that this supernatural event took place in an everyday setting i.e., a wedding, demonstrates that God is not limited to performing miraculous events in church. Rather, they can infuse our daily lives. Several thousand years may have passed since that first miracle, but God is still in the business of taking the plain 'water' of our lives and turning it into high quality 'wine'—transforming the ordinary into the excellent.

---

57 Jesus gave many demonstrations of his superiority over Old Testament prophets, even when it came to food. In 2 Kings 4:42-44, the prophet Elisha feeds one hundred men with twenty loaves of bread. Jesus fed over five thousand people starting with only five loaves and two fish (Mark 6:35-44).

PETER NETS A NEW JOB

Nachman Koppelman
Office of the Harbour Master
Sea of Galilee

Simon Peter
The Fisherman's House
Capernaum

Date: A.D. 27

Dear Simon Peter,

I've noticed your fishing boat has been tied up for so long that its marina tags have expired. What's going on, Peter? Did you get a little tipsy one night and forget where you moored your boat? Under the terms and conditions of a commercial mooring, a fishing boat must be in regular use, and it's obvious to all concerned that yours isn't. It has that abandoned look about it. If you've indeed given up fishing—and rumours suggest you may have done just that—I can arrange to change you over to a public mooring instead. That way, your boat can sit unused and unloved, bobbing up and down on the waves for as long as you keep paying the monthly fee.

Have you really turned your back on your fishing career? The story I heard was that after an unsuccessful night fishing with Andrew, someone called Jesus appeared. He borrowed your boat to preach from, then told you to take your boat back out into deeper water and throw your nets out. You reluctantly followed his instructions and ended up catching so many fish the nets were breaking.[58] Then, after one of your largest and most successful catches ever, you gave it all up to follow him. Talk about impulsive! I wouldn't want to go giving you a sword—who knows what you might do with it.

---

58 Luke 5:4-6

I believe Jesus also said he would make you 'fishers of men'. Fisher of men, fishing for men, men in fishnets—it all sounds very dubious. What about fishing for fish, or am I asking too much? If you do intend to 'fish for men', may I remind you that catching men for the slave market without an official permit is seriously frowned upon by Rome. Be aware that should any of the lifeguards observe you trying to catch people, especially those swimming between the flags, they will notify the authorities immediately.

Jesus certainly sounds like a slave trader to me; tell me, have you checked out his background or asked the police? I also heard he might have a drinking problem, as he arrived at a wedding in Cana with over five hundred litres of wine—or something like that. You're making a mistake here, Peter, a big mistake. Fishing has a future, and eating fish will never go out of fashion. Whatever this Jesus is doing, I can assure you, it has no future and never will.

Also, it appears you abandoned your nets without cleaning them, and now other marina users are complaining about the smell. I swear I got a whiff of it coming through my office window last week—that, or someone dropped something dead off the end of the wharf. Anyway, unless you resume using your boat or relocate to a public mooring, your boat and gear will be seized and sold. I'm afraid you need to attend to this matter urgently as there is a waiting list of fishermen keen to take over your spot, especially with it being so close to Maria's lunch bar. Did I mention she's just added fish toasties to the menu?

I'm told you have an excellent reputation as a fisherman. It would be a shame to throw it all away to follow whatever crazy scheme Jesus is promoting. Think it over carefully, Peter. You're a fisherman, not a slave trader, and career changes this late in life—they never end well.

Yours,

Nachman Koppelman
Harbour Master

DISCUSSION

A MOTLEY CREW OF DISCIPLES

Jesus chose twelve men to become his closest disciples—men he would instruct and train up to take the gospel into the world. Before they got started, Judas Iscariot betrayed Jesus and committed suicide, and James—the brother of John—was put to death sometime around A.D. 44 by Herod Agrippa I (one of five people called Herod in the Bible).

Peter, Andrew and brothers James and John (Matthew 4:18-21) are all listed as fishermen. James and John are described as "sons of thunder" (Mark 3:17), suggesting a certain volatility in personality. The pair were all for calling down fire from heaven and destroying the residents of a village in Samaria because they hadn't given Jesus a warm and friendly welcome (Luke 9:54). Such nice chaps.

There was also Matthew (or, Levi—Mark 2:14), who had been working for the Roman authorities as a tax collector, and Simon the Zealot. ('Zealot' is believed to be a reference to a political group opposed to the Roman occupation.) Next up was Thomas, who was often labelled "doubting Thomas"[59] because he didn't initially believe Jesus was alive again when he first heard the news. Which is worse, I wonder, doubting Jesus's resurrection or wanting to incinerate a village?

Through his choice of disciples, Jesus demonstrated he could make use of people with a wide range of backgrounds and character flaws, and clearly he knew a thing or two about personnel management. Ultimately, the kingdom of God cares less about our abilities and more about our heart attitude. Concerning salvation, God doesn't play favourites—only faith is required.

HOW MUCH IS ENOUGH?

There are those who believe there is an alternative to this faith-based salvation approach, and it involves being a good person or doing good things. If we accept, for a moment, this 'good people go to heaven' philosophy, then we must ask ourselves: How much 'good' does one need to do? Is there some performance standard or measurement that needs to be met? If this was the case, the Bible would have to include a scale so we could keep track of our score. Otherwise, we would be forever living in uncertainty, wondering if we've 'made it in'. Also, what if two people did the same good deed but one gave it a higher value than the other? A fixed scoring system would be necessary in order to prevent people over or undervaluing their efforts. We would also need to know how many bad deeds it would take for us to have our entry to heaven

---

59 Despite this incident, Thomas is believed to have eventually taken the gospel message as far as southern India. Today there are a number of churches in India named after him, especially in Kerala State in the South West.

disqualified.

Similarly, some people assume that being financially generous will enable a person to reach heaven. If this were indeed a viable alternative, the logical question would be: How much must a person give away or pay to meet the required threshold? This raises a number of additional questions, including:

- Can I pay what's required as a lump sum, or must I make regular ongoing payments?
- Is it a fixed price? Does someone in 2020 have to pay the same as someone in 1960—or put another way, is inflation factored in?
- What about people who work the same job but get paid different amounts, leaving one with more to give away than the other. Is this somehow 'balanced out' in the end?
- Is a fixed dollar amount required from each person, or is it calculated proportionally according to income?
- Can charitable donations be split between different groups, or do some charities score higher on the 'heaven scale'?
- Can I transfer surplus money to someone else to give them a 'leg up' into heaven?

Finally, if you really can buy or donate your way into heaven, why would Jesus say it is harder for a rich man to enter heaven? (Mark 10:25). Surely it would be harder for a *poor* person to enter heaven—unless of course, you can't buy your way into heaven in the first place.

SALVATION BY FAITH

There is a reason we don't find within the Bible any form of points scale for getting into heaven. Instead, it declares salvation is by *faith* and not by works:

> For it is by grace you have been saved, through faith—and this is not from yourselves, it is the gift of God—not by works, so that no one can boast.
> Ephesians 2:8-9

Salvation by faith alone levels the playing field. It disregards race, wealth, circumstances, age, and mental and physical capability. In fact, the length of life one has left to live is irrelevant. A person who is near death in a hospital or hospice is at no disadvantage compared to a young healthy person, and neither is the poor person at a disadvantage compared to a rich person.

What the salvation-by-good-deeds approach fails to recognise is the personal transformation that occurs through faith-based salvation where Jesus begins a process to change us from the inside out. A 'good person', in the worldly sense, may never have gone to church, read a Bible, sung a Christian song, heard a sermon preached, learnt about Jesus, or asked for forgiveness for their sin. They may have done plenty of good things in their life but remain unchanged where it matters most. If such a person could enter heaven, they might bring along with them some very unpleasant personal traits which would certainly make it a little (or a lot!) less appealing for everyone else.

BUSINESS ADVICE FOR JESUS

Cohen, Stern & Steinbach

Lawyers, Accountants and Business Advisers

3rd Floor, Jerusalem Plaza

Jesus of Nazareth

The Fisherman's House

Capernaum

Date: A.D. 28

Dear Jesus,

A colleague recently drew my attention to your new enterprise operating as a soul trader. When I reminded him that sole traders were too small for us to be involved with, he emphasised you weren't a sole trader but a *soul trader*. To be frank, it all sounded the same to me—perhaps you can explain the difference to me one day. Then, the news came through that you'd increased the size of your venture by taking on twelve assistants, followed sometime later by a further seventy-two staff.[60] Cohen, Stern & Steinbach have experience with large staff groups including King Herod's palace and the Sanhedrin, so you'll be in good hands should you decide to work with us.

It's been reported that your catering division provided food at very short notice for around five thousand people. This is very impressive indeed, especially as those in attendance remain completely mystified as to how you did it. I've done a little background research into your operation, and I see you started out dabbling in wine-making. After

---

60 Luke 10:1 Around half of old manuscripts say 70, the other half say 72.

that, you moved into the fishing industry. Despite achieving early success in this area, you subsequently talked the fishermen into signing up for something more religious in nature. Expansion soon followed into the teaching, medical, and social justice fields. I'm pleased to say that yours is definitely the type of operation Cohen, Stern & Steinbach would be proud to be associated with. We stand ready to assist in any way we can—though, of course, modest fees would apply.

We offer a full range of financial and business services along with professional legal advice, all of which can be tailored to your specific requirements. We are able to provide offshore accounts, foreign exchange, and set up shell companies. If need be, we can register your operation in Germania,[61] which falls outside the tax jurisdiction of the Roman Empire, making every dollar you earn a tax-free one.

I was unable to find your organisation's operating capital and share structure at the Business Registry Office. One comment claimed your finances were 'faith-based', which sounded a little like money turning up out of thin air. Just to be clear, money turning up like that isn't looked upon favourably by auditors.

If you would like more information, I can have the High Priest provide you with a personal testimony of our efficiency and business acumen. It was our suggestion that money changers be allowed into the Courtyard of the Gentiles in the temple. After all, God is hardly interested in gentiles, and the space seemed to be going to waste— though thanks to us, not any longer. It brings a certain satisfaction knowing that, on this occasion, we were helping to do God's work.

Yours

Arron Cohen
Cohen, Stern & Steinbach

---

61 Modern-day Germany.

DISCUSSION

WHAT'S IN IT FOR ME?

As Jesus became better known, his popularity among the general population began to rise. On the other hand, his preaching didn't always go down well with existing religious leaders, especially when he highlighted their flaws and shortcomings (Matthew 23:27-28).

There were many who mistook and misunderstood what Jesus was trying to achieve, and rather than focusing on spiritual issues and the kingdom of God, they (like the fictitious Cohen, Stern & Steinbach) were more interested in what was in it for them personally. They sought immediate and worldly gratification rather than the spiritual and eternal blessings Jesus could offer them. One example of this occurred the day after Jesus's miraculous feeding of the five thousand. When the people tracked Jesus down, he told them they hadn't come because of the miraculous healings they had seen him do but rather because he had provided them with food to eat (John 6:22-26). Unfortunately, there'll always be those only in it for the freebies.

MOTIVES MATTER

Whenever God moves and things begin happening, those with wrong motives will inevitably be drawn in also. Smooth talking and personal flattery are nothing new, as Paul notes:

> *I urge you, brothers, to watch out for those who cause divisions and put obstacles in your way that are contrary to the teaching you have learned. Keep away from them. For such people are not serving our Lord Christ, but their own appetites. By smooth talk and flattery they deceive the minds of naive people.*
>
> *Romans 16:17-18*

For those to whom God has given the responsibility for operating various ministries, it is important to determine the true motives of people who want to share in the work. Those more interested in seeking their own wealth, influence or recognition will hinder the effectiveness of a ministry and could even destroy it or bring it into disrepute. When it comes to kingdom work, the devil loves getting the wrong people slotted into the wrong places. People trying to 'steal the limelight' is not unique to Christian activities, but such behaviour can certainly have a detrimental effect on God's work in the world.

During the Welsh Revival, which broke out in the United Kingdom between 1904-1905, over

100,000 people came to know Christ.[62] However, the central figure—twenty-six-year-old Evan Roberts—soon became heavily influenced by a Mrs. Jessie Penn-Lewis, who provided him with accommodation while he recovered from mental strain. As the revival progressed, she wielded progressively more control over his life, decisions and actions, while at the same time using his high profile to further her own publications and ministry. Dr. Roberts Liardon (author, public speaker, and church historian) noted in his 1996 book *God's Generals—Why They Succeeded and Why Some Failed:*

> "In my opinion, it seems that Mrs Penn-Lewis was using the strength and call of Evan Roberts to promote herself. From past record, she didn't have the strength, character, or call to make it on her own . . . If she could gain his partnership, then she could share his platform."[63]

Ideally, the church would only do good works without letting greed, lust and corruption get in the way. Unfortunately, we live in a sin-filled world, and sin is deceitful—very deceitful—to the point where it is capable of tripping up even those who have been in the faith for many years.

> *But encourage one another daily, as long as it is called "Today," so that none of you may be hardened by sin's deceitfulness.*
> *Hebrews 3:13*

The lure of money, sexual lust, recognition, power, drugs and alcohol all stand ready to trip up leaders and ruin lives and ministries given the slightest opportunity. The devil doesn't mind how high you climb, so long as you fall off at the top—even better if you take people with you when you come crashing down. In addition to these traditional stumbling blocks, one might also add faulty and compromised theology and conspiracy theories. I think Paul nailed it when he wrote this ancient yet oh-so-modern advice to Timothy:

> *For the time will come when people will not put up with sound doctrine. Instead, to suit their own desires, they will gather around them a great number of teachers to say what their itching ears want to hear.*
> *2 Timothy 4:3*

---

62 www. revival-library.org/histories/1904-welsh-revival. A revival is a significant visitation of God's invisible presence that draws the saved and unsaved to repentance and quickens the hearts of existing believers. It usually involves prayer, salvation of the lost, repentance, and sometimes healing, although each revival has its own unique signature. A revival can last from weeks to years.

63 *God's Generals—Why They Succeeded and Why Some Failed.* Whitaker House. Reprint edition. Albury Pub 1996. © Roberts Liardon. (p98)

THE SAD STORY OF THE HARD-DONE-BY FINANCE MEN

Temple Stall Holders Association
Chamber of Commerce
Jerusalem

Joseph Caiaphas
High Priest
Jerusalem

Date: A.D. 28

Dear Joseph,

Yesterday an ugly incident occurred in the Courtyard of the Gentiles where money changers and animal sellers were subjected to a violent attack at the hands of a mad man. He ran around shouting, making wild claims about family ownership of the temple, turning over tables, and causing general pandemonium—all of which scared animals and sellers alike. Many of the traders ran in fear for their lives, and half didn't return to work the following day. I've been in contact with Cohen, Stern & Steinbach here in Jerusalem who explained that, by allowing my members to be exposed to the danger they were in, the temple may be in breach of a number of Roman Laws, including:

- Demonstrations and Protesters Act
- Turtledoves and Pigeons Animal Welfare Act
- Unrestrained Animals In Courtyards Act
- Religious Safe Spaces Act (Amendment IV)
- Foreign Exchange Dealers Regulations (Denarius Transactions)

The culprit is a man called Jesus, who I understand has previously stirred up trouble in other parts of the city. He arrived in the Courtyard of the Gentiles armed with a whip of cords and highly agitated. As the money changers were going about their business helping those arriving for Passover, Jesus let loose. As soon as his whip started cracking, the animal sellers panicked, coins went flying, and cage doors were flung open. Within moments, the air was thick with whirling doves. Have you ever had pigeon poo in your eye, High Priest? I assure you it is most unpleasant.

Worse still, some of the larger animals broke loose and began a stampede, resulting in high-pitched, frantic screaming coming from the Courtyard of Women. At least I think it was, though it's possible the high-pitched, frantic screaming may have come from the Courtyard of Priests—I find the two can sound quite similar. One gent from Rome had a most unfortunate encounter with a goat horn and is now unlikely to ever father children again. On the bright side, another man who experienced a similar incident will now never need to have his appendix removed.

Believe me when I tell you it was utter pandemonium with goats, sheep and cattle running and colliding with people and one another. This resulted in the unblemished livestock becoming very blemished indeed and, as a consequence, quite useless for sacrificing. Did I mention the cattle dung? My goodness, I never knew scared cattle could, you know, poo quite so freely and so often. The stuff can be truly lethal when you're running, too—slippery as ice, it is. It turns out it also sticks to clothing like glue and certainly isn't pleasant should one have the misfortune of falling into some—I speak from experience.

Above all the screaming and shouting on the day, I just managed to catch Jesus saying that his father owned the temple. I ask you, what sort of person goes around making a claim like that? I'll leave you to sort it out, it being your temple and all. I'm fairly sure that if you check the ownership documents, his father's name won't be anywhere to be seen. In addition, he said the place where he was standing (the Courtyard of the Gentiles) was for prayer, not commerce, and all the traders had to leave. Stall holders pay a handsome commission for the privilege of operating in that space, and they're feeling let down by the lack of intervention by the temple guards. Need I remind you that all this occurred during Passover celebrations? If people no longer feel safe coming to Jerusalem at this busy time of year, we will all feel the financial effects of lower turnouts, and you'll collect far less temple tax.

I have enclosed an account covering the total cost, which covers damage to cages, injured and blemished livestock, torn robes, escaped doves, drycleaning, and money that 'helpful' gentiles picked up on the day but 'forgot' to hand back in. I'm confident you can deal with the matter swiftly without my members having to resort to making a claim under the Business Disruption Act.

Yours very concerned,

Ira Goldstein
Senior Partner

DISCUSSION

JESUS'S TEMPLE TAKEDOWN

Two different accounts of Jesus cleansing the temple are recorded in the Gospels. The first occurs at the start of Jesus's ministry during Passover (John 2:13-16). The second (in the Matthew, Mark and Luke Gospels) occurs during the last week of Jesus's life. Some believe all four accounts cover the same event, while others believe there were two separate events around three years apart. The point highlighted in both accounts is how Jewish leaders had allowed the Courtyard of the Gentiles to be transformed from an area of prayer into a commercial one.

CORRUPTION IN THE COURTYARD

People were required to purchase animals for use in sacrifices (even Jesus's parents made such a purchase in Luke 2:22-24), so it wasn't the sale of animals or the involvement of money that was a problem. What was problematic was the location of this commercial activity. It is also likely that corruption was involved—perhaps through the use of unfair exchange rates or inflated animal prices. Another possibility is that those who brought their own sacrificial animal were being told the animal wasn't suitable (even though it was) and, instead, were made to purchase one in the temple.

The idea that some form of corruption was occurring in the temple is suggested by Jesus himself when he quoted from Jeremiah 7:11 in the Old Testament. Some translations swap 'robbers' for 'thieves'.

> *"It is written," he said to them, "'My house will be called a house of prayer' but you are making it 'a den of robbers.'"*
>
> *Matthew 21:13*

A NECESSARY MONETARY EXCHANGE

Why *was* money being exchanged? Apart from making it easier for those from foreign lands to use local currency for purchases, there was a requirement for people to pay the temple tax.[64] It was originally instigated by Moses (Exodus 30:13-16) as an annual payment for the upkeep of the tabernacle—a giant tent where the people used to worship God before the First Temple was built by Solomon, King David's son. When the tabernacle was replaced, the tax continued and was applied to the temple's upkeep instead.

In Matthew 17:24-27, Peter is challenged about whether Jesus pays the temple tax, and, without first checking with Jesus, he answers that he does. Jesus sends him out to catch a fish which turns out to have a single (Tetradrachm)

---

64 Temple tax for 1 person = ½ a Tyrian shekel = 2 Roman drachmas. Temple tax for 2 people = 1 Tyrian shekel = 4 Roman drachmas (a Tyrian shekel was also known as a Tetradrachm, Tetra=four, so four drachma).

coin in its mouth. Peter uses it to pay the tax for both of them. Fishy tax payments clearly aren't something new.

It has also been said that Jewish leaders didn't want to deal with the Roman-minted coins that carried an image of the emperor, signifying Rome's authority. Instead, they required payment be made with Tyrian shekels and half-shekels that didn't contain any Roman imagery. On the other hand, those coins displayed an image of the pagan Greek god Heracles, which would have been just as offensive to the Jews. Another common reason given for this required exchange is that Tyrian shekels and half-shekels were made with a more reliable and accurate quantity of silver, thus in accepting them, the temple ensured it wasn't being short-changed. Whatever the real reason may have been, the temple would only accept payment in Tyrian shekels or half-shekels, and worshippers were required to exchange their money accordingly.

DISADVANTAGED AND DISTRACTED

It is estimated that up to several hundred thousand people came from outside Jerusalem to attend the annual Passover festival. Consequently, many people would be disadvantaged by any financial wrongdoings by the money changers. Even if they and the animal sellers were trading honestly (which is doubtful), they were definitely doing it in the wrong location. Their operations were interfering with worship taking place in the Courtyard of the Gentiles, as worshippers were likely distracted by the crowds around the money tables, the smells, animal noises, and the talking and shouting of the traders.

Interestingly, the First Temple, sometimes called Solomon's Temple, didn't have a Gentile's Courtyard while the Second Temple, also known as Herod's Temple after King Herod had undertaken a major decades-long renovation project on it, did.

TITBITS FROM THE TRADERS

Meanwhile, in a corner of the Courtyard of the Gentiles:

"Change your drachmas here, best rates in Jerusalem!"

"Buy ten shekels get a free autograph from the High Priest!"

"Tyrian shekels, half-shekels—three tables operating, no queueing."

"Buy four shekels, get a half-price turtle dove."

"Get your Tyrian shekels now, all foreign coins accepted!"

"Shekels, shekels, more shekels than you can shake a sheep at!"

JESUS'S CARE FOR THE GENTILES

In short, something was happening at the temple that shouldn't have been, Jesus was onto it, and he called them out over it. The majority of those attending Passover would have been Jews, but there would have been gentiles there also, and it was important they had the space and the opportunity to worship God as well. The Old Testament contains numerous references to God's interest in and provision for the gentiles, and this action by Jesus in protecting their courtyard only highlighted that provision further. When we get to the Book of Acts, Peter has a vision which turns the whole Jew/gentile issue upside down (Acts 10:9-16).

TRICKY QUESTIONS FOR JESUS

Gideon Raziah

Chief Priests Discussion Group

Joseph Caiaphas

High Priest

Jerusalem

Date: A.D. 28

Dear Joseph,

Last week at the meeting of chief priests and teachers of the law, you outlined to those present the many problems Jesus of Nazareth has been causing and called for fresh solutions. After discussing the matter further, my group has come up with the idea of asking Jesus tricky questions while he is out in public. He is bound to give a wrong answer eventually, and we'll be able to use that to discredit his teachings. It doesn't necessarily even need to be a wrong answer; he might say something the people don't like or that puts him in conflict with the Roman authorities, leading to his arrest or even execution.

I have outlined three possible questions below which I am confident will bring the outcome we all seek.

Is it right to pay the imperial tax[65] to Caesar or not?

If Jesus answers the tax *should* be paid, then the people will see him as a supporter of

---

65 Mark 12:13-17. This was a Roman tax, not the local temple tax.

the Romans and their occupation. He'll become as unpopular overnight as a blocked sewer. On the other hand, if he says people *shouldn't* pay the Roman tax, we can report him to the authorities for rebellion against the Roman State. If that happens, he's likely to be executed. Personally, I can't see how things could go wrong. He can only give two answers: pay or don't pay. Either way, it will be a win for us. Is it too soon to be opening wine to celebrate?

Should he somehow wiggle his way out of that one, then we move onto question two. A Sadducee will ask about marriage responsibilities and what happens at the resurrection (not that the Sadducees believe in the resurrection of course, but they are just as keen to get rid of Jesus as we are and will be glad to help out). Their question will be:

If a woman's husband dies and leaves no children, and she then marries the next brother in line but he dies—and so on and so on through all seven brothers—whose wife will she be in the resurrection?[66]

She can't have seven husbands at the same time in the resurrection because she would be committing adultery, which is a sin. Alternatively, rather than permit sin to happen, Jesus will have to deny there is any resurrection after death which will go against his own teachings as well as what we as Pharisees believe. He'll be cornered—either he'll have to support adultery taking place in the resurrection or be forced to deny his own resurrection teachings. We can't possibly lose. Another glass of wine, High Priest?

If Jesus is able to answer his way out of those two tricky questions, and it's unimaginable how he could, we will move onto the big gun. We will stage a set up involving a woman and a man, burst in and catch the two in the act, then drag the woman to Jesus.[67] We'll remind him what the Law of Moses says about punishing an adulterer and then stand back and see what he does. We'll be sure to have plenty of rocks close by so he can start stoning her straight away, and there will be those of us ready to join him once he gives the go-ahead. He can't possibly get out of this one—absolutely no way. If he says not to stone her, then he'll be letting adultery go unpunished. And if he's not following the Law of Moses, he's clearly not sent from God as he claims to be.

---

66 Mark 12:24-27
67 John 8:1-11

If, however, he says to stone her—or stones her himself, which I hope he does—then people will see he supports the law that *we've* been teaching. He will be seen as either a law-breaker or a law-supporter, and the hope people have placed in him will be dashed either way. It is surely only a matter of time before our problems with Jesus are over. Do you prefer red or white wine, High Priest?

Regards,

Gideon Raziah

DISCUSSION

CONFLICT BETWEEN JESUS AND THE RELIGIOUS LEADERS

When Jesus arrived on the scene and suggested the religious leaders of the day weren't doing things the way God had intended and that their interpretations of the law were distorted, they became very angry with him. From then on, the religious elite were constantly on the lookout for ways to trap and trick Jesus so they might discredit and stop him. On the odd occasion, they even plotted to kill him (Mark 3:6).

A TROUBLESOME TAX

In his answer, Jesus doesn't specifically endorse Caesar (the emperor) nor comment on the Roman occupation of the land. Instead, he tells those listening to continue giving to Caesar what they are required to give (their Roman tax) but, just as importantly, to give to God the things he asks for. The first item on God's list is our heart.

> *My son, give me your heart and let your eyes delight in my ways.*
> *Proverbs 23:26*

Once God has our heart, we will be more willing to do the other things he asks of us. The things of this world (government, money, and possessions) are temporal—that is, only for a time—whereas the things of God are spiritual in nature and eternal in duration. Christianity has practical teachings that help us to live in the here and now, but its ultimate focus is on a future where sin, death and corruption are not present.

Score sheet: Jesus 1, Temple Tricksters 0

RELATIONSHIPS IN THE RESURRECTION

Religious groups in Jerusalem at the time of Jesus included the Sadducees and Pharisees (there were also the Essenes). Their beliefs differed slightly but, in particular, the Sadducees didn't believe in the resurrection and the Pharisees did. The Sadducees who asked Jesus this question may have hoped he would confirm their belief there was indeed no resurrection. Secondly, even if the resurrection was true, they wondered how Jesus would deal with a woman who had gone through seven husbands while alive on earth.

Jesus answered in two ways. Firstly, he confirmed the resurrection, which would have been a disappointment for the Sadducees for sure. Secondly, by saying marriage doesn't exist for those who have been resurrected (Matthew 22:23-33), he implied the married status of a person on earth doesn't continue on into heaven.

Score sheet: Jesus 2 — Temple Tricksters 0

MERCY OR JUDGEMENT?

Since only the woman was caught in the act of adultery but not the man, it was evidently a set-up. Jesus doesn't revoke or cancel the requirements of the Law of Moses for her to be stoned, instead, he points out that all who are present are sinners too. Then, he invites anyone who hasn't sinned to throw the first stone. Jesus doesn't excuse the woman but tells her not to sin anymore, which suggests she had actually committed adultery.

Of those standing around waiting for the stoning to begin, the older people leave first, perhaps more quickly recognising their own sinfulness. Eventually, everyone else follows, after realising they, too, are equally guilty before God of one sin or another. Interestingly, Jesus—who was sinless and, according to his own teaching, was the only one who could have stoned her—extended mercy to her instead of punishment.

Score sheet: Jesus 3 — Temple Tricksters 0

A QUESTION OF AUTHENTICITY

For many, the events recorded in this passage exemplify 'classic' Jesus—holding true to the Law but adding new depth and compassion to it. However, the authenticity of John 8:2-11 has been debated over the centuries due to its inclusion in some early copies of Scripture but not others. Most Bibles highlight this discrepancy with footnotes, italicised text, or something similar.

WHAT DID HE WRITE?

This passage notes that Jesus wrote something on the ground—the only time Scripture ever records this. What did he write? Some have suggested it could have been a list of the sins of all those who were accusing the woman.

One also wonders if his mother came to mind as he was writing. As a young woman, Mary's pregnancy began before her marriage to Joseph, and, in the eyes of the religious leaders, she too would have been guilty of adultery under the Law and worthy of being stoned.

KNOW YOUR BIBLE

People often twist Scripture for their own benefit or to defend an incorrect doctrine. The better we know our Bible, the more effective we can be in recognising error and deceit. Three times the religious leaders tried to trap Jesus using Scripture deceitfully, and three times Jesus used his superior scriptural knowledge to rebut them.

PETER'S INSURANCE CLAIM

Capernaum Fire & General Insurance Co.

Head Office

New Siloam Tower

Peter

The Fisherman's House

Capernaum

Date: A.D. 28

Re: Insurance Claim For Damaged Roof

Dear Peter,

I have just finished reading your claim in which you state a hole appeared in the roof of your house as a result of "a group of men making an opening to lower down a man on a stretcher."[68] This 'hole' doesn't sound like accidental damage to me. You also say an 'Act of God' was occurring inside your house at the time. Clearly your view of an *Act of God* differs from the one used by Capernaum Fire & General Insurance Co. It certainly doesn't mean you can claim God did something in your house and hold us financially responsible for any associated damage.

What you're talking about here sounds far more religious in nature. You wrote, "Jesus was in the house doing God's work." If that is indeed true, then I suggest you take it up with the High Priest at the temple in Jerusalem. I can't imagine him being anything less than fully supportive and prepared to help out, even as far as covering any costs to repair your roof. After all, he—and the other religious leaders—represent and work for God, do they not? Or are you daring to suggest their actions may be hindering religious progress around these parts?

---

68 Mark 2:1-12; Luke 5:17:26

Our company assessor has examined the hole and finds you in breach of a number of policy conditions. Specifically, these are:

Clause 3.8: Property occupancy not to exceed thirty people.

In case you have forgotten, you live in a house, not the Circus Maximus. Naturally, we don't object to you having a few friends around, but if you don't know the difference between five and ninety-five, we suggest you buy yourself one of those clicker counter things or employ a bouncer.

Clause 18.6: Steps must be taken to immediately prevent further damage.

What happened exactly? You saw a small hole appear in the ceiling and thought, *I can't see that getting any bigger,* so you left it? Or perhaps holes regularly appear in your ceiling and this one, much to your surprise, grew rapidly to an unusually large size—large enough that a stretcher could be lowered through it. However it happened, it is clear you did nothing to prevent it.

Clause 22.2: Wilful damage is *not* covered by this policy.

This hole was no accident, and it is therefore not covered by the policy. The men who made the hole are vandals, Peter. It is as simple as that.

Clause 27.4: Un-notified structural alterations not covered.

All homeowners undertake minor repairs and maintenance—it's something I do myself. However, replacing a broken brick or applying a new coat of whitewash is quite different to making *structural alterations.* They are named as such as they help hold the house together, including the roof of your house. A large hole in it makes it structurally unsound and risks total collapse. Since you don't have a public liability policy, you should consider yourself fortunate the roof didn't cave in and kill someone.

Please note that Capernaum Fire & General Insurance Co. must be notified of all structural changes in advance, and all work must be undertaken by a suitably qualified craftsman. I understand that Jesus is—or was, prior to his religious crusade—a carpenter. Did you not think to consult him about the hole and the danger it might pose to those in attendance?

Clause 29.1: Policy only covers normal domestic activities.

Capernaum Fire & General Insurance Co. pride themselves on taking a flexible approach in their definition of normal domestic activity. However, lowering a stretcher through one's roof far exceeds even our generous view of 'normal'. Do your neighbours engage in this sort of unusual behaviour? I thought not, which proves my point.

I am also confident the Insurance Council will support our view that by having Jesus—a well-known religious person—conducting a meeting with well over thirty people present, what you were actually doing at the time was operating a synagogue. In order to have insurance coverage for that, you will need to purchase a Religious Buildings and Activities Policy. If you think you are likely to continue with these religious meetings, I could have one of our agents call on you with the policy wording for you to take a look at. You should be aware that even this type of policy *does not* cover people making a hole in your roof. No insurance policy does, because such an action is vandalism.

For all of the above reasons, your claim is denied.

Yours sincerely,

Artemis Prometheus
Manager

DISCUSSION

JESUS STAYS WITH PETER

After Jesus moved from carpentry into full-time ministry, many believe that while he was in the northern part of the country, he based himself at Peter's house in Capernaum.

> *A few days later, when Jesus again entered Capernaum, the people heard that he had come home.*
>
> *Mark 2:1*

Upon his arrival, Jesus first heals Peter's mother-in-law from a fever. The next morning, Jesus gets up and leaves Peter's house, so he obviously stayed for one night at least.

> *Very early in the morning, while it was still dark, Jesus got up, left the house and went off to a solitary place, where he prayed.*
>
> *Mark 1:35*

A 'HOLE' LOT OF TROUBLE

We know Peter had a wife but her view of the roof event is not included in the biblical account. We also don't get to hear how she felt about Peter's career change from fisherman to religious trainee. The following *might* be a conversation they had, though probably not:

"Darling I'm home. I've got big news!"

"What is it?"

"I'm changing jobs—no more fish smells."

"You're giving up fishing?"

"I am indeed. I'm joining Jesus and helping him with his spiritual stuff."

"Spiritual stuff? Have you lost your mind?"

"No, I haven't, I thought you'd be pleased."

"Pleased? Why would I be pleased? You'll just end up just like those temple people . . ."

"Oh no, it's nothing like that. What we'll be doing is travelling around and . . . "

"Who's we?"

"Me, Andrew, and some of the others. There's twelve of us plus Jesus."

"You just *had* to go and talk your brother into joining you, didn't you?"

"Andrew seemed keen."

"Just like you talked him into becoming a fisherman. How far will you be travelling?"

"Look, I'll get Jesus to explain it. He'll be here soon, he's coming to stay."

"Stay? Stay where?"

"Stay here with us."

"Have you forgotten my mother's sick? Now you want me to sort out accommodation for this Jesus!"

"If you could . . . Is there a problem? Darling, say something . . . you're going very red in the face . . . now you're going blue . . . breathe . . . please breathe. Look, I'll clear out those old fishing nets from the storeroom, and your mum can sleep in there. Jesus can have her room . . . Put the knife down, I was only joking about the storeroom. We'll sort something out, I promise."

"And is Jesus going to help with groceries?"

"I'll ask him. I know he can cook[69] so you might be surprised at how far he can make a couple of loaves of bread and a fish or two go."

"There better not be any damage to the roof, Peter. If the roof gets damaged, I'll . . ."

"Damage to the roof? What on earth makes you think Jesus staying here is going to result in damage to the roof?"

"I don't know, I've just got this funny feeling."

Whether Peter held further meetings in his house is unknown, and the one involving the hole may have been a one-off. I've always wondered if, after the meeting, Jesus helped to repair it: "Don't worry about the hole in the roof, Peter. I've fixed hundreds of them in my time." Or perhaps he said, "I'm off to preach in the next town, hope you get the hole fixed before I get back—it looks like it might rain later."

THE BLESSING OF MARRIAGE

Peter's wife appears to have not only been a believer but accompanied him at times as he travelled around preaching. Paul refers to this in 1 Corinthians 9:5 (NB: Peter was also called Cephas):

> *Don't we have the right to take a believing wife along with us, as do the other apostles and the Lord's brothers and Cephas?*

Although the Catholic Church has promoted singleness and celibacy for its Pope and priests, the Protestant church holds to no such teaching. The Catholic Church views Peter as the first Pope even though Peter was married. Historically, it appears the celibacy requirement within the Catholic Church became standard around the 11th Century. Paul is viewed by most scholars as being single (1 Corinthians 7:7), and while he wrote on the merits of singleness, he also taught a lot about marriage and its blessings. The Bible even gives us a warning that the day will come when some will teach against getting married.

> *They forbid people to marry and order them to abstain from certain foods, which God created to be received with thanksgiving . . .*
>
> 1 Timothy 4:3

THE COST OF CHRIST

Following Jesus often comes with a cost, although it usually doesn't involve the roof of one's house being partly demolished. Then again, in some countries church buildings have been torn down or burned by groups or governments opposing Christianity.[70] As difficult as it may be to pay such a price for our faith, it pales in comparison to the blessings which wait for us in eternity (Romans 8:18).

---

69 After Jesus's resurrection, some of the disciples came ashore after fishing to find a fire going and cooked fish and bread ready for them to eat. Since Jesus was alone on the shore (although the disciples did not initially recognise him), it is likely he was the one who cooked the meal (John 21:9-12).

70 https://www.ohchr.org/en/press-releases/2023/09/india-un-experts-alarmed-continuing-abuses-manipur

MORE INSURANCE PROBLEMS FOR PETER

Capernaum Fire & General Insurance Co.
Head Office
New Siloam Tower

Peter
The Fisherman's House
Capernaum

Date: A.D. 28

Re: Reassessment of Your Insurance Claim

Dear Peter,

I see you wrote to the Insurance Fairness Inspector attempting to convince him you had a valid insurance claim for your roof under sub-clause 86-5 of your policy. Capernaum Fire & General Insurance Co. disagree. I have written to the Insurance Fairness Inspector myself to tell him as much and to reiterate we won't be paying out any compensation. You are, of course, free to live your life how you please. On the other hand, Capernaum Fire & General Insurance Co. has no obligation to pay up when religious activities get out of hand and your house gets damaged.

I am sorry to hear that you didn't have any success getting the High Priest to pay for your roof repair. I guess he agreed with our view of an 'Act of God'—not your imaginative interpretation of it. By the way, have you tried sharing your 'Jesus is God' ideas down at the temple? I hear they are still waiting for the arrival of the promised Messiah, and the Jesus you described in your claim sounds as though he may well be the man they're after. I'm sure they couldn't be anything but delighted to hear this directly from you in person.

I know our policy document has rather a lot of pages all written in very small text—we use six-point-size Insurance Policy Font. Naturally, we would be happy to use a larger-sized text, but this would use up far more paper—paper made from the endangered papyrus reed. Instead, as a responsible corporate member of society, we view using a small-sized text as our contribution to helping secure the planet's future. It certainly isn't intended to make reading your policy uninviting or difficult but is solely a planet-saving effort.

You told the Insurance Fairness Inspector that the hole wasn't, in fact, connected to the religious meeting but rather "had been made to assist in providing urgent medical treatment to a man in desperate need of assistance." You therefore hoped it would be covered under sub-clause 86-5: Use of house parts for providing emergency medical assistance/treatment.

I'm afraid you are mistaken. Coverage under this clause applies *only* when it becomes necessary for parts of your house to be used in the medical procedure itself—for example, using a wall baton to splint a broken bone or roof thatching to stem the flow of blood. Unfortunately, since the hole in your roof only allowed the patient *access* to treatment, it isn't covered.

What I fail to see is why the man wasn't just carried inside through the front door. Was it broken, or did you lock it and lose the key? Was entering the building through the roof part of some religious ritual? Did the person have to appear to 'float down from the sky' or be presented horizontally as though they were a sacrificial offering on an altar? I warn you, Peter, this religious business you've got yourself involved with is likely to end up costing you more than a roof repair.

For the above reasons, your claim is *still* declined, and we are cancelling your policy.

Yours sincerely,

Artemis Prometheus
Manager

DISCUSSION

STANDING ROOM ONLY

According to the account in the Gospel of Luke, people had come from far and wide to attend the meeting in Peter's house (Luke 5:17). This wasn't just a few friends getting together to drink wine and discuss religious scrolls—in other words, a home group or Bible study. Rather, the meeting included religious top brass from as far away as Jerusalem (roughly 120 kilometres from Capernaum) along with a mix of local attendees. The house was packed—standing room only—and one couldn't get in the front door even if one wanted to.

> They gathered in such large numbers that there was no room left, not even outside the door, and [Jesus] preached the word to them.
>
> *Mark 2:2*

THE ROOM WHERE IT HAPPENED

Fire safety regulations didn't appear to be a big thing back then but being packed into a house like sardines in a tin can clearly was. As Jesus preached, the Pharisees likely squirmed in their seats—as the Pharisees often did when Jesus preached. Until pieces of ceiling began falling on top of them . . .

"Hey Peter, you need to get your roof fixed! A piece just fell on my head and almost knocked me out."

"Yeah, Peter, I'm covered in white stuff, and now I look like I've got dandruff."

"You didn't tell us you were having a skylight installed."

"Does your wife know about the skylight? Peter . . . she doesn't, does she?"

"Peter, you're going to get into so much trouble for not telling her."

As more of the roof disappears, other voices can be heard from above:

"Watch out, even it up . . . pull up on your corner . . . quick, he's tipping . . . we don't want to kill him before Jesus prays for him! Oh bother, his sandal's fallen off."

JESUS DEMONSTRATES HIS AUTHORITY

As people look up, they see a bed containing a paralysed man being lowered on ropes. The faces of four men peer into the room from above, looking down at the man now lying in front of Jesus. They are expectant, they have faith, and they care about their friend. They don't care about Peter's roof. The Pharisees—who have given up squirming in their seats for a moment—lean forward, watching with interest. Jesus subsequently tells the man his sins are forgiven which, although it's a nice thing to be told, is probably not what his friends were expecting—and certainly not what the Pharisees expected to hear as only God could forgive sin. Here, Jesus is treading on very thin theological ice, and the teachers of the Law are not impressed.

Now some teachers of the law were sitting there, thinking to themselves, "Why does this fellow talk like that? He's blaspheming! Who can forgive sins but God alone?"

Mark 2:6-7

Jesus had a surprise for them. He not only forgave the man his sins but healed him also, demonstrating he had the full authority of God.

HOLDING ONTO FAITH

As with the men and their bedridden friend, stepping out in faith is often not only about choosing to believe God despite the circumstances, but it may include a practical component, too. In order to reach Jesus, the man's four friends were required to carry their friend all the way to the meeting. They then had to climb up onto the roof—probably via an external staircase that many houses had back then—and remove enough tiles to lower him through the resulting hole (Luke 5:19).

Faith often requires us to hold onto nothing more than the promise of God. We may have to stand by, waiting and watching, as our circumstances don't line up with our expectations. When the men arrived, they found entry to the house blocked by those at the door. Yet instead of giving up, they headed to the roof. When they heard Jesus say that their friend's sins were forgiven, did their hearts sink? Was there really to be no physical healing—the reason they had brought him along in the first place?

It's so easy for our faith to begin to falter if a situation gets worse—as a person's vital signs start to decline or if, day after day, the doctors say there's no change. Sometimes things may even get worse after we first venture out in faith, but if God has promised us something, he is faithful and he will come through. When the doctor says there's only a five percent chance, God responds, "That's plenty, I can do it with only one percent." And when God delivers on his promise, we can rest assured that all the tears, the emotional pain, the anguish, the stress and worry our soul has been through become worth their weight in gold.

JESUS AND THE JERUSALEM MEDICAL COUNCIL

Jewish Medical Council [JMC]

Temple Precinct

Jerusalem

Jesus of Nazareth

C/- Mary, Martha, and Lazarus' House

Bethany

Date: A.D. 29

Re: Practicing Medicine Without a Licence

Dear Jesus,

The Medical Council has been made aware of numerous allegations against you regarding your practice of medicine here in Jerusalem and elsewhere without a licence. If this is indeed true, it is both a very serious accusation and highly unethical. Further, your style of medicine—if we can indeed call it 'medicine'—is of particular concern given your lack of formal diagnostic testing and use of unconventional treatment methods. One is left wondering about the source of these so-called 'healings', or if it is just—as many have suggested—outright trickery.

We have an eyewitness who claims you used human spit on a patient during a consultation. He maintains you mixed *your own spit* with dirt, made mud, and smeared it on a man's eyes. Fortunately, being blind he didn't see it coming. Then, you declared his sight was restored.[71] I don't know what, if any, medical training you may have had, but it is

---

71 John 9:6-7

my experience that mud rubbed into eyes usually causes problems, not solves them. The man did end up being able to see afterwards, but in the absence of an eye test beforehand, there's no way of reliably knowing if he was ever truly blind. Even some of his neighbours seem to have been uncertain on this point.[72]

In another case, it is claimed you healed ten lepers at the same time! Ten at once? What were you trying to do, gain an entry in Noah's Book of Records for the most patients seen in a single consultation? Given such a large group consultation, there are additional concerns you may have failed to maintain patient confidentiality. For example, how did you ensure the condition of each patient was not disclosed to the others?

The Council also has no record of you attending any professional development classes. How do you expect to keep up with current treatment options if you never show up? Much of what you pass off as medicine appears to be far more about religion and God. You need to be clear: medicine is medicine, religion is religion. If you keep mixing up the two, we'll end up with people wandering the streets of Jerusalem saying, "God healed me."

There are numerous reports that you claim to have healed people from leprosy, insanity, and even physical deformity. I have to ask: Is there any condition you can't heal? The best doctors in Jerusalem struggle to treat with any level of success even a fraction of the conditions you've tackled. To hear you've healed people suffering from all of them is, quite frankly, unbelievable. God himself might be able to manage it but no one else can—of that I am certain. Is there any possibility that you are God? (A Pharisee called Nicodemus suggested I ask you.)

Allowing people to believe you have done something which we all know is medically impossible is not only an insult to the Hippocratic Oath[73] but a breach of medical law. It is also having a rather negative effect on the income of local doctors, with some experiencing a drastic drop-off in cash flow and patient numbers. Your style of medicine is also potentially very harmful to patients, as they could easily slip into

---

72 John 9:8-11

73 An early ethical oath (4th century B.C. or earlier) sworn by new doctors. Since updated from the original and still in use today. Attributed to Hippocrates, a Greek physician (460–370 B.C.).

a depression when they discover they aren't really cured and you aren't a real doctor. Admittedly, there are a few people who will believe anything a person tells them—like that unfortunate chap in the Gerasenes[74] region who was nutty as a fruitcake and known to walk around naked. It was good of you to get him to put his clothes back on, but as for him thinking he was cured, well, that's another delusion on his part. While it is true he is still talking and behaving normally and remains fully clothed (once again, thank you for that), it is surely only a matter of time before he relapses.

I understand you have a number of disciples, and the last thing the Medical Council wants to see is any of them following in your footsteps. The city has enough health issues as it is, and there is no room in Jerusalem or elsewhere for medical slight of hand mixed with religious mumbo jumbo. As part of due process outlined in the JSG Medical Act (Judaea, Samaria, and Galilee), we require you to attend a hearing of the Jerusalem Medical Council next Monday after morning prayers where you can answer all the charges against you.

I strongly suggest you avail yourself of legal counsel. In that regard, Cohen, Stern & Steinbach here in Jerusalem may be able to assist. The sooner your medical make-believe comes to an end, the safer Jerusalem will be.

Yours,

Dr Gershom
Jerusalem Medical Council Chairman

---

74 Luke 8:26-37

DISCUSSION

POWER OVER THE PHYSICAL WORLD

Jesus provided many different proofs that he was the Messiah—the anointed one—in human form. One way he did this was to demonstrate his power over the physical world, including:

- Water into wine (John 2:1-11)
- Multiplying food (Matthew 14:18-20)
- Calming a storm (Luke 8:22-24)
- Walking on water (Matthew 14:24-27)
- Defying gravity (Acts 1:6-11)

EVIDENCE THAT JESUS IS THE MESSIAH

Jesus also demonstrated his power over sickness, disease, and demonic spirits. In Luke 6:17-19, we read about a huge crowd of people, many of whom were sick and in need of delivery from impure spirits, who came to hear Jesus preach. Though easily overlooked, this account is perhaps *the most dramatic* demonstration of mass healing in the entire New Testament. It also mentions that people from Tyre and Sidon (both non-Jewish cities) were present in the crowd which would make it one of the few times in the gospels that we see the healing power of God poured out on the gentiles.

. . . and a great number of people from all over Judea, from Jerusalem, and from the coast of Tyre and Sidon, who had come to hear him and to be healed of their diseases. Those troubled by evil spirits were cured and the people all tried to touch him, because power was coming from him and healing them all.

Luke 6:17-19

After Jesus returned to heaven, this same healing power continued to flow through the apostles.

Crowds gathered also from the towns around Jerusalem, bringing their sick and those tormented by evil spirits, and all of them were healed.

Acts 5:16

Note that healing wasn't anything the apostles themselves could do, rather it was divine power operating and flowing *through them* that brought healing. This holds true today. We must be mindful of the fact that those praying for the sick have no healing power of their own, rather it is the power of God flowing through them, just as it flowed through the disciples.

The following list includes cases of healing by Jesus which involved individuals or small groups:

- Ten men with leprosy (Luke 17:11-17)
- A paralysed man (Matthew 8:5-13)
- A woman with a fever (Matthew 8:14-15)

- A man with a withered hand (Matthew 12:9-14)
- A woman who had a discharge of blood for twelve years (Matthew 9:20-22)
- A man who was mute (Matthew 9:32-33)

Modern medicine has made much progress and is able to bring relief to those suffering from a wide range of conditions. As Christians, we can thank God not only for modern medicines but diagnostic equipment such as MRI[75] and CT scanners. Despite these medical advances, however, some conditions—including paralysis, advanced cancers (especially pancreatic and liver), and complex brain tumours— currently remain beyond our ability to cure. Yet even two thousand years ago, such conditions were no match for Jesus. He even healed blindness (John 9:1-6; Matthew 9:27-29; Matthew 20:29-34).

RESTORING LIFE TO THE DEAD

Even if modern medicine advances to the point where it can cure even the most complex conditions, restoring life to a corpse remains in the 'God only' department.[76] Nevertheless, Jesus performed it several times:

- The twelve-year-old daughter of a synagogue's leader (Luke 8:49-56)
- A man called Lazarus, who was dead three days (John 11:32-45)
- A widow's only son (Luke 7:11-15)

WORTHY OF OUR WORSHIP

For many, these demonstrations of his power provide clear evidence that Jesus was God. Yet he did all these things *and* was able to forgive people their sins. Paul writes in Philippians 2:9-11 that Jesus has been exalted to the *highest place* and given a name *above all others*. He is the one to whom *every knee will bow,* and every tongue will confess that he is Lord. The Father has entrusted all judgment to Jesus (John 5:22), and we are told in Hebrews 1:4 that he is superior to *all* angels.

When the disciple Thomas called him "God" (John 20:28), Jesus didn't deny it nor rebuke him in response. In fact, he was worshipped by multiple people on multiple occasions including the wise men (Matthew 2:11), the disciples (Matthew 14:32-33), the two Marys (Matthew 28:9), and a blind man whom he healed (John 9:38). At no point did Jesus rebuke any of them for worshipping him, and yet Jesus himself said: "It is written: 'Worship the Lord your God and serve him only'" (Luke 4:8). Jesus was either sinning when he accepted the worship of others, or he was God in human form and therefore worthy of receiving it.

Jesus had authority over the demonic spiritual realm, the physical earthly realm, over the laws of physics and chemistry, and

---

75 As it so happens, the invention of the MRI scanner is credited to Raymond Damadian, a Christian. www.icr.org/article/raymond-damadian-inventor-mri

76 Nowhere in Scripture do we read of any created being (human or angelic) restoring life to another. When this power was demonstrated by a prophet or one of the disciples, it was always given by God in prayer.

demonstrated power over all demonic forces he encountered. He also said, "Anyone who has seen me has seen the Father" (John 14:9), and for that to be true, Jesus would have to be an exact representation of the Father—so much so that you couldn't tell them apart. This is exactly what the Bible claims.

> The Son is the radiance of God's glory and the exact representation of his being . . .
> *Hebrews 1:3*

WHO IS JESUS IF NOT GOD?

We do not read of any angel having the power to create, bring back life, or forgive sin, nor may angels accept any worship (Revelation 19:10), yet Jesus did all of these. If one disagrees that Jesus is indeed God, then there are two questions that need to be answered:

1. Who exactly *is* Jesus if he is not God?

2. How can he be an *exact* representation of God the Father without being divine himself?

MONEY CHANGERS

Cohen, Stern & Steinbach
Lawyers, Accountants & Business Advisers
3rd Floor, Jerusalem Plaza

Jesus of Nazareth
The Fisherman's House
Capernaum

Date: A.D. 28

Dear Jesus,

At the close of my previous letter to you, I made mention that we had provided advice to the High Priest concerning money-changing operations at the temple complex. It has come to my attention that you recently expressed your disapproval of the presence of the money changers and animal sellers operating there. Your intervention sounded quite dramatic, what with overturned tables and such.

I'm sure your actions were quite justified, although not being a temple-going man myself, the ins and outs of the religious side of things are a little beyond me. My main concern is that the comments I made at the close of my letter aren't taken the wrong way. So easy to get the 'wrong end of the stick', as they say. I therefore felt it best to write and clarify our involvement.

It is true that the Chief Financial Officer (CFO) for the temple approached Cohen, Stern & Steinbach seeking advice regarding expanding the temple's income streams. *More money for God*, I thought, *what could be wrong with that?* After an on-site visit, we provided the High Priest with a few ideas—mere suggestions, really, hardly anything at all. I'm surprised the man couldn't have thought them up himself.

For a start, when the team visited, they noticed the Courtyard of the Gentiles wasn't operating at capacity. This led to the misunderstanding that the area was more or less available for uses other than solely religious ones. Clearly—as we now know—that was not the case. As I said, here at Cohen, Stern & Steinbach we aren't really temple-going people, so some of the deeper religious aspects may have been a little lost on us. In hindsight, we should probably have engaged a consultant ourselves, someone knowledgeable on religious matters—maybe even one of your men. I understand Judas Iscariot has an interest in doing jobs to earn extra money.

Anyway, last on the list of suggestions was one about providing a small money exchange service for those coming for the Passover festival. Something very discreet. A small operation tucked away in some far corner, where out-of-town visitors could exchange money for the temple tax. Unfortunately, the High Priest seems to have taken our best intentions and turned them into something far grander—in this case, the extensive foreign exchange and animal-selling operations you came across on your visit.

I must emphasise that any implementation of the suggestions was entirely at the High Priest's discretion. Had we known the importance you attach to having an area fully dedicated to gentiles (one unincumbered with the trappings of commerce), we would never have made the suggestions we did. Never—you have my word on that. Please accept my personal apologies for the unfortunate outcomes our work led to. I trust this helps to clear up any misunderstanding regarding our involvement.

Yours,

Arron Cohen
Cohen, Stern & Steinbach

DISCUSSION

In the middle of Jerusalem stood the Jewish temple complex, the focus of religious and national life. King Herod had begun renovations around 20 B.C. and these were ongoing, even during the time of Jesus.

THE SCOPE OF THE TEMPLE RENOVATIONS

They replied, "It has taken forty-six years to build this temple, and you are going to raise it in three days?"

John 2:20

Forty-six years refers to how long the restoration work had already been in progress, as final alterations were not complete until some decades later. The Temple Mount was a precinct that comprised a paved plaza area, walls, gates and entrances, arches, and the like. Upon this sat the temple itself. The Temple Mount covered an area of around 140,000–150,000 square metres (approx. 37 acres). It was a piece of ground roughly 380 by 380 metres. In short, it was large and dominating.

GENTILE ACCESS TO THE TEMPLE

The temple complex contained four courtyards, one of which was used by gentile believers. This was the only area where non-Jews were allowed, and it was divided from the inner areas of the temple. Several inscriptions written on stone blocks that were once present in the temple courtyard have been found. They contain a warning to outsiders or non-Jews against entering the temple enclosure on pain of death. At one stage, Paul was falsely accused of allowing gentiles to cross over this dividing barrier into the Jewish area.

When the seven days were nearly over, some Jews from the province of Asia saw Paul at the temple. They stirred up the whole crowd and seized him, shouting, "Fellow Israelites, help us! This is the man who teaches everyone everywhere against our people and our law and this place. And besides, he has brought Greeks into the temple and defiled this holy place." (They had previously seen Trophimus the Ephesian in the city with Paul and assumed that Paul had brought him into the temple.)

Acts 21:27–29

Is it just me or does this sound a lot like how many people on social media operate these days? They see or hear something, but without investigating, assume something has or hasn't happened, is or isn't true, then react and tell the world.

COMMERCIAL ACTIVITY IN THE COURT OF THE GENTILES

Jews were allowed into the gentile courtyard, along with pagans. But when it came to the Jewish areas, there were restrictions. Keep in mind that it was mostly Jews who were buying animals for sacrifice and needing to change money to pay the temple tax. At some stage, money changers and animal sellers had set up their operations, but was this done in one of the areas set aside for Jews? Not at all. They set up shop in the gentile courtyard. When it came to courtyards, the gentiles were outnumbered three to one, and their one courtyard was partly overtaken by commercial activity. Effectively, those involved in the activity were commercialising access to God.

The money and animal operations no doubt made the space noisy, smelly, and at times quite crowded, such as during Passover. Come festival time, hundreds or maybe thousands of Jews would have entered the Court of the Gentiles, done business, and then left. All of this would have made it more difficult for gentiles to worship God and to pray. In fact, in one account, this was a primary complaint of Jesus, that prayer was being impeded.

> "It is written," he said to them, "'My house will be called a house of prayer,' but you are making it 'a den of robbers.'"
>
> *Matthew 21:13*

GOD'S DESIRE FOR THE GENTILES

The fact that the temple required a dedicated area be set aside for gentiles is further evidence of God's long-term plan for humanity, a plan that would include all people, Jews and gentiles alike. God's desire was to open the gates of salvation to the gentiles, and when Paul explained this in his letter to the church in Rome, he quotes from the book of Hosea (2:23):

> "I will call them 'my people' who are not my people; and I will call her 'my loved one' who is not my loved one," and, "In the very place where it was said to them, 'You are not my people,' there they will be called 'children of the living God.'"
>
> *Romans 9:25-26*

THE END OF TEMPLE DIVISIONS

With the death of Jesus, everything to do with the temple was about to change. The old system of animal sacrifices, the temple, priests, and courtyards would come to an end. What appeared to be an exclusive deal between God and the Jews was about to be turned on its head. Soon, God would welcome anyone who calls on his name, Jew and gentile alike.

> . . . remember that at that time you were separate from Christ, excluded from citizenship in Israel and foreigners to the covenants of the promise, without hope and without God in the world. But now in Christ Jesus you who once were far away have been brought near by the blood of Christ.
>
> *Ephesians 2:12–13*

CAREER ADVICE FOR JESUS

Cohen, Stern & Steinbach
Lawyers, Accountants and Business advisers
3rd Floor, Jerusalem Plaza

Jesus of Nazareth
The Fisherman's House
Capernaum

Date: A.D. 28

Dear Jesus,

Some years back, a man called Theudas came along claiming to be a religious somebody. He started well enough by gathering around four hundred followers[77] but then ended up dead as a religious nobody. I ask you, how much good can the death of a man—no matter how religious he may be—really bring to others? I say none whatsoever unless, of course, the person who dies was some sort of sacrifice—and surely you aren't promoting human sacrifice, are you? One person dying for the whole world would truly be quite a feat. To start with, where would you possibly find someone who's lived a life perfect enough to pull that off? I can assure you it won't be any of the people I associate with—especially after what happened last weekend in Beersheba. Their women sure know how to drink and party.

Anyway, religious stuff is your department, but I think you're making the wrong career choice. What exactly is it that you think you can bring to the religious landscape that doesn't already exist? The Jews have taken over downtown Jerusalem with their enormous temple complex which is constantly crawling with devoted adherents. They've also got that big annual Passover festival which attracts large crowds from near and far. On top

---

77 Acts 5:36

of that, they've got the largest collection of ancient written scrolls I've seen anywhere. Whatever way you look at it, you have a lot of competition to contend with.

To have any chance of succeeding you definitely need some religious writings of your own. If you do decide to write something, a word to the wise: don't go including stories like that one about the prophet Nehemiah. He finds out that some men had married foreign women and their kids couldn't speak Hebrew. Unhappy about the situation, he responds by calling curses down on them, beating some of them up, and pulling out their hair.[78] Something tells me an approach like that is going to make it hard to win converts. I'd recommend cutting your followers a bit of slack—offer them a new deal, more food choices, a more flexible attendance schedule, maybe fewer laws and regulations to follow, and an easier way to sort out obtaining forgiveness. Something involving fewer animals dying should be a winner.

Not to put too fine a point on it, you haven't written anything and, of course, you don't have a temple. A much better idea, in my view, would be to give up the religious business entirely and move into catering. Start by supplying food and beverages for weddings and festivals—you'd be great at it. You could call it 'Water to Wine Catering' or, if you decide to target the business market, 'Loaves and Fishes after Five'. Leave religion to the Sadducees otherwise, if you put them out of a job, they might end up sad, you see. They're already a glum bunch without you adding to their misery. I mean, the poor things don't even have an afterlife to look forward to.[79]

Your water-into-wine technology gives you a great competitive advantage and would allow you to make product fresh on-site. This would save significantly on storage and transportation costs and, in turn, increase profit margins. Just think of the fortune that could be made from taking water (still free from the Jordan River last time I checked) and turning it into wine to sell.

In addition to the wine thing, I'm told you also have a process that can rapidly multiply food. Talk about having the God-touch. Next, I'll be hearing you can calm storms,

---

78 Nehemiah 13:25

79 The Sadducees (as opposed to the Pharisees) didn't believe in the afterlife or the resurrection of the dead.

cure multiple lepers at a time, get crazy people to put their clothes back on, and cure blindness using mud pies. With this food-multiplying technology, one could give some consideration to solving world hunger, a worthy cause for sure. Better still, think of all the money you could make. Ever fancied a gold-plated chariot or—with the fortune you could make—a solid gold one?! You might just need to buy a few extra horses to pull the thing.

I suggest you follow my advice and leave the religious stuff to those at the temple—trust me, they have things well under control. As always, please feel free to call in at our offices and come in for that chat.

Yours,

Arron Cohen
Cohen, Stern & Steinbach

DISCUSSION

COMMISSIONED FOR THE KINGDOM

Back in the early 1990s, bracelets bearing the letters WWJD became popular amongst Christian youth. The letters stood for the question: What Would Jesus Do?[80] But what about WDJTUTD: What Did Jesus Tell Us To Do?

Jesus gave Christians two important jobs: the first being to preach the gospel—the good news of the kingdom of God.

He said to them, "Go into all the world and preach the gospel to all creation."

Mark 16:15

The second job, sometimes called "the Great Commission," involves making disciples of those who come to Jesus. Those who respond to the gospel need to be discipled in the faith.

Jesus said . . . "Therefore go and make disciples of all nations, baptizing them in the name of the Father and of the Son and of the Holy Spirit, and teaching them to obey everything I have commanded you."

Matthew 28:19-20

EQUIPPED FOR THE CALL

Mercifully, God provides people with a range of spiritual and natural talents which allow each of us to perform different roles as we assist in undertaking this important kingdom work. Some will work on the 'front line' and others in support roles. Some will be seen publicly, and others will labour behind the scenes—perhaps caring for others or interceding in prayer. Yet, God sees all and keeps score.

Some will shine brightly and become well known, or even famous globally or within their specific field. However, we each have a responsibility to be good stewards of the gifts God has given us, and as far as he is concerned, worldly fame is just a byproduct of advancing his work in the world.

From everyone who has been given much, much will be demanded; and from the one who has been entrusted with much, much more will be asked.

Luke 12:48

Swiss-born Leonhard Euler (1707-1783) was not only one of the world's greatest ever mathematicians (Euler's Identity, anyone?), but he also used his intellect to defend Christianity.[81] Eric Liddell, well known for his Christian faith and refusal to compete on Sundays, won gold at

---

80 What Would Jesus Do? From the book *In His Steps* published in 1896 by Rev. Charles Sheldon.

81 www.breakpoint.org/leonhard-euler-called-to-mathematics, www.christianperspective.net/blog/leonhard-euler

the 1924 Paris Olympics.[82] Yet his faith perhaps shone most brightly when away from onlookers and cheering crowds. It motivated him to serve the needs of fellow prisoners during the three years he spent in a Japanese internment camp in Weihsien, China, during WWII. He died there in 1945 from a brain haemorrhage.

Talented linguists translate the Bible into obscure languages. Then there are those who have trekked for days or weeks through jungles to live with tribal groups and teach them about Jesus. Others, including Mission Aviation Fellowship (MAF), help out by flying planes and landing them on jungle airstrips so people no longer have to trek through jungles.[83]

Sadly, a few fly planes and end up speared to death on a river bank deep in the jungles of Ecuador. It doesn't happen often, but it did back in 1956. Nate Saint, although your life was short, your dedication inspired thousands of others to sign up to take your place and advance the kingdom of God. Then, it happened again in 2018. Although he wasn't a pilot, it was nevertheless a tragic ending to what was always going to be a dangerous (and controversial) undertaking by John Chau who visited the isolated North Sentinel Island in the Indian Ocean to share the message of Jesus but was killed by the inhabitants upon arrival.

COMMITTED TO THE CAUSE

God anoints, blesses and enables people to advance the work of his kingdom. Seeing it at work, non-believers sometimes try to re-direct it for other purposes. One of my favourite evangelists was William (Billy) Franklin Graham Jr. (1918-2018). No, I never met him in person, and, yes, he had his faults. Make anyone your hero, and one day you'll end up disappointed after discovering they aren't as perfect as you thought they were.

From 1947 to 2005, he held large meetings known as crusades, where audiences typically numbered in the tens of thousands or greater. He was the first-known evangelist to preach live to an audience of one million people face to face. One person who thought Billy's God-given talents could be redirected was the then President of the United States. One day while swimming together at Camp David, President [Lyndon] Johnson said in front of a group of people, "Billy, you ought to be president of the United States. If you do run, I'd like to be your campaign manager." Billy laughed and said, "You're joking." Johnson replied, "No, I'm serious. I mean it."[84]

---

82 Born in China to Scottish missionary parents. The 1981 film *Chariots of Fire* depicts part of his life's story. His gold was for the 400m event.

83 https://www.maf.org. JAARS (Jungle Aviation And Relay Service) are similar to MAF but also work with boats and land vehicles: www.jaars.org

84 www.billygraham.org/story/trivia-what-political-office-was-billy-graham-encouraged-to-run-for/

Fortunately, Billy knew God had called him to preach the gospel and only preach the gospel, and he remained faithfully committed to that task despite other generous offers. One might ask, *What Would Jesus Do?* and come to the conclusion that since political decisions can affect an entire nation, Billy should have entered politics. Yet laws and regulations don't resolve humanity's fundamental problem: the sinfulness of the human heart.

> *The heart is deceitful above all things and beyond cure. Who can understand it?*
> Jeremiah 17:9

WILLING TO SERVE

Mankind has been in moral rebellion against God since people decided to go their own way back in the Garden of Eden. Political policy, laws, self-improvement classes and 'positivity' programmes are solutions the world offers to the problem of human sin. Yet it is only Jesus who can bring true inner renewal and transformation through spiritual rebirth. In the 1980s, the United States Marine Corps ran a series of recruitment advertisements using a tag line that went something like: "The Marines: We're looking for a few good men." I don't know if they found them, but God is still looking for anyone with a willing heart to serve and build his kingdom.

WE ARE TAKING YOU OFF OUR CLIENT LIST

Cohen, Stern & Steinbach
Lawyers, Accountants and Business advisers
3rd Floor, Jerusalem Plaza

Jesus of Nazareth
The Fisherman's House
Capernaum

Date: A.D. 29

Dear Jesus,

I have tried, genuinely tried, to understand your life choices, but they continue to utterly confuse me. Your ability to produce food and wine in the blink of an eye could make you enormously wealthy but you choose not to make money from it. You've cured every known disease and yet do not set yourself up as a man of medicine. You pursue religious matters despite having no writings or temple in a marketplace flooded with other religions. Where has this religious obsession got you after three years? Nowhere. In fact, you've had as much impact as a cup of salt added to the Dead Sea.[85]

What puzzles me most is that you've gone to all this effort when there's really no need. People already have dozens of Greek and Roman gods they can choose from, including Zeus, Poseidon, and Aphrodite. There are also temples built to these gods all over the place, and in addition, the Jews have their own one here in Jerusalem. The one particularly odd thing about the Jewish one is that it doesn't contain an image of

---

85 The Dead Sea contains so much salt that one floats in its water rather than sinks.

134

their God.[86] The interior is just open space, a few ornaments, and a large fancy curtain. Furthermore, people worship outside the temple, not inside—did someone forget it rains in Jerusalem? They also don't offer any carved or moulded miniatures of their God for sale. Don't you find that odd, or is it just me?

Perhaps you're thinking of exporting your religious ideas if you ever get some momentum, but even here I think you'll struggle. You see, the Persians have Zoroastrianism,[87] and there's Hinduism, Buddhism, Sikhism and Jainism as well. Anyone else in your position would have given up and gone home long ago. To beat the competition, you'll need to pull off something big and do it soon, or you'll end up out of time. None of us are promised forever.

For what it's worth, I'll give you credit for persistence. It's as though you believe millions of lives depend on what you're doing. Have you considered that it might be your teachings that are holding back progress? Long sermons on mountain tops[88] might not be crowd pleasers. And think about the prostitutes working at the various temples and shrines—if they were to follow your teachings on sexual fidelity, it would mean instant unemployment for the lot of them. You need a message that fits with the culture of the day, something that doesn't require people to give up all of their vices. People don't want to be lectured on sin, that's for sure.

A lot of the ideas you promote are confusing, and that's putting it mildly. Take, for example, the talk of being sent by God whom you say is your Father. That one's gone completely over my head, sorry, because I always thought Joseph was your father. I even looked you up on the birth register, and it definitely had Joseph's name written down. You also said you are the Bread of Life and people had to eat it—that is, they had to eat you. While your audience struggled with that idea, and I can see why they might, you upped the stakes by saying that whoever ate your flesh and drank your blood[89] would have eternal life. Too much, Jesus—way, way too much. It's no surprise you're

---

86 Exodus 20:4-5

87 Zoroastrianism was founded in Persia (roughly modern Iran) approximately 3500 years ago by religious prophet Zoroaster (Zoroaster is the Greek version of Zarathustra).

88 Known as the Sermon on the Mount, covered in Matthew chapters 5-7.

89 John 6:53-66

losing followers. These are hard concepts to grasp.[90] If you ever do decide to go into catering after this, I fear such comments may permanently damage your reputation. Eating food promoted by someone holding positive views on cannibalism is always going to be a tough sell.

Unfortunately, you and I have reached the end of the road. Eating your flesh and drinking your blood, and all that talk of destroying the temple, exceed even what Cohen, Stern & Steinbach can cope with. I am now withdrawing my offer of providing any further assistance, not that you ever took up my offer of assistance to begin with. I just can't see what you're doing ever becoming a success. It could have all been so different but, sadly, perhaps some things just aren't meant to be.

At this point, your only possible hope of success is if you were fulfilling a master plan designed by God himself, and I'd have to be crazy to believe that. Even if that were the case, it's the strangest master plan I've ever come across. No temple, no writings, only twelve core followers, and several long-established major religious systems competing against you. Sorry, Jesus, it will never work—not even if you die trying. In two thousand years, I seriously doubt anyone will ever know who you were or what you did.

Yours,

Arron Cohen
Cohen, Stern & Steinbach

---

90 John 6:60-66

DISCUSSION

GOD'S WAYS ARE UNFATHOMABLE

God is God, and we are not. It's a fairly obvious distinction although there are those in psychiatric institutions and the odd dictator here and there who, from time to time, think otherwise. It's no surprise then, God chooses to do things differently to how we would.

As the heavens are higher than the earth, so are my ways higher than your ways and my thoughts than your thoughts.

Isaiah 55:9

Scripture also reveals that those who haven't been born anew by the Spirit of God don't understand God's spiritual ways.

The person without the Spirit does not accept the things that come from the Spirit of God but considers them foolishness, and cannot understand them because they are discerned only through the Spirit.

1 Corinthians 2:14

JESUS'S EARTHLY OBJECTIVE

The methods Jesus employed while on earth— the things he did and said, interactions he had with people, and what he chose to teach—may come across as an odd way to establish a major world religion. Not that establishing a religion was his main objective. Rather, he was intent on making it possible that sinful people could be reconciled back to God the Father. Each person's sin breaks the spiritual link to God.

As for you, you were dead in your transgressions and sins.

Ephesians 2:1

Through salvation in Jesus, that link is re-established (this is known as being born again or renewed by the Spirit of God), and we are reconciled or put back in right relationship with God the Father.

Therefore, if anyone is in Christ, the new creation has come: the old has gone, the new is here! All this is from God, who reconciled us to himself through Christ and gave us the ministry of reconciliation.

2 Corinthians 5:17-18

THE COST OF OUR CONVICTIONS

Those who are not believers will at times not understand why you choose to do the things you do or value the things you do. They may even cut off contact once they discover you have become a Christian, or treat you differently. Family members, a previous friend or a work colleague might become hostile despite having been friendly towards you for years. Giving up one (false) religious system in order to believe in Jesus may generate hostility from those who continue to maintain your former beliefs. Such a response is primarily a reflection of their hostility towards Jesus, which he warned us about. This can be a challenging thing to deal with and work through.

> *"If the world hates you, keep in mind that it hated me first. If you belonged to the world, it would love you as its own. As it is, you do not belong to the world, but I have chosen you out of the world. That is why the world hates you.*
>
> *John 15:18-19*

FINDING OUR TRUE WORTH IN CHRIST

There are only two spiritual kingdoms—one of darkness and one of light. Everyone starts life in the kingdom of darkness because all have sinned (Romans 3:23). However, we enter, or are adopted, into the kingdom of light at the moment of personal salvation.

> *For he has rescued us from the dominion of darkness and brought us into the kingdom of the Son he loves.*
>
> *Colossians 1:13*

As we mature in Christ,[91] those things we previously valued and held dear will become less so. Paul reached a point where he saw most things as less than worthless.

> *What is more, I consider everything a loss compared to the surpassing greatness of knowing Christ Jesus my Lord, for whose sake I have lost all things. I consider them garbage, that I may gain Christ.*
>
> *Philippians 3:8*

The NIV translation is being modest when it uses the word 'garbage'. In my view, Paul's feeling is better expressed in the King James Version which uses the phrase: "count them but dung." The word 'garbage' gives an impression of worthlessness, but 'dung' adds a sense of revulsion. One might still keep a broken toy on a bookshelf even though it's worthless, yet one wouldn't keep a lump of dog dung. If you are keeping lumps of dog dung on your bookshelf, please seek help.

Note: Keeping dry cattle dung to use as a fuel source for your home stove is fine—you don't need to seek help for that.

---

91 In life, aging is compulsory, maturity is optional. Unfortunately, not everyone who begins a Christian walk matures in it. Paul referenced this when writing to the church at Corinth. They had members who had been Christians for some time, but who had failed to advance and were still needing help to understand basic principles (1 Corinthians 3:1-2).

JUDAS SEEKS LEGAL ADVICE

Judas Iscariot

C/- No Fixed Abode Hostel

Jerusalem

Cohen, Stern & Steinbach

Lawyers, Accountants, and Business Advisers

3rd Floor

Jerusalem Plaza

Date: A.D. 30

Dear Sirs,

I am one of the twelve disciples chosen by Jesus to work alongside him. There have also been several women helping out behind the scenes with fundraising,[92] cooking, and other such work. I am writing to you today to seek your advice, as my co-workers and I are regularly exposed to workplace dangers but have never received any financial compensation. Take the case of the man from the Gerasenes, for example, who was out of his mind, naked, and running amok. People had previously tried chaining him up, but he would always break free.[93] Despite knowing this, Jesus took us to visit him anyway. Fortunately, on that occasion we all survived, but you can clearly see this is a risky lifestyle we are forced to live.

Then, there was the time Jesus *slept* while the rest of us were in great peril. We were twelve good men in a boat on a lake in the middle of a ferocious storm. Waves were lashing the sides of the vessel, and soon water was flooding over the gunwales, swamping

---

92 Luke 8:1-3

93 Mark 5:1-13

the boat and threatening to sink it.[94] As we edged ever closer to perishing, what did Jesus do? Nothing. He kept on sleeping. Once again, we were fortunate to survive our ordeal. Were we given financial compensation afterwards or offered counselling to deal with the trauma of it all? None whatsoever.

Almost daily we put our lives on the line. Recently, we were out doing a spot of house-to-house visiting and ended up at Simon the leper's place.[95] "Unclean, unclean!" I shouted, but Jesus took no notice and made us go inside. Leprosy is an incurable disease, you know. People die from it. You can understand my frustration at the situation, to say nothing of the stress and anxiety it caused me. And then, while we were there, a woman broke open a jar of perfume and poured it over Jesus.[96] It seemed to me a weird way to treat a guest, but that's not the half of it! She didn't use any of that cheap stuff like 'Midnight In Damascus' which you can buy in the back street bazaars and smells much like Peter's unwashed feet. No, what *she* used was made from nard, no less, and must have been worth at least a year's wages. If she didn't want it, I could easily have sold it for her, and my commission rates are more than reasonable.

The stupid thing is, Jesus said the woman poured the perfume out to prepare him for his burial—which came as a real surprise since he hadn't told any of us he was sick. If he really was dying then I could have accepted it, but days have passed and, as far as I know, he's looking no worse now than he did back then. Jesus does that from time to time—he says odd things that leave us wondering if he might be losing the plot. Are we compensated for the public embarrassment we suffer? Not at all. What we get instead is exposure to infectious diseases and having our opinion disregarded while valuable goods are squandered.

Jesus keeps telling the team that great riches await us in heaven as a reward for our hard work. That is all well and good, but my concern is, given the state of the economy these days, heavenly riches mightn't be worth quite so much by the time I get there. *So, why not take an advance,* I thought to myself, *like what an author gets from a publisher,*

---

94 Matthew 8:23-27

95 Matthew 26:6. It is unlikely Simon had active leprosy as this would have made him unclean. It's more likely he had been healed from it, probably by Jesus, but the name 'leper' stuck.

96 Mark 14:3-9

then collect the rest on arrival after I die? I subsequently decided to 'reallocate' a sum of money from the group funds in order to make a few purchases here and there—nothing fancy you understand. I was going to mention it to Jesus but he's a busy man, and I could never quite find the right time.

In another attempt to improve my financial position, I came to an arrangement with the chief priests and secured payment of thirty pieces of silver in exchange for providing inside information about Jesus's whereabouts.[97] After realising this wasn't such a good thing to have done, I went back to return the money, but they refused to accept it. Hypocrites! They rush to take your temple tax off you but won't accept a refund when you try and give them one.

In your opinion, should I be concerned about the funds I reallocated from the money bag? I think I may have kept some receipts if that would help, and I'm sure some of the extra items I purchased qualify as tax deductible. At least, they do according to the Roman Tax Code, section VII—I checked that with Matthew. He used to be a tax collector you know. Please advise me as soon as you are able.

Yours,

Judas Iscariot

---

97 Matthew 26:14-16

DISCUSSION

WHAT'S IN A NAME?

Even though today the name Judas is strongly linked with a sense of betrayal or being a traitor ("You told on us, you Judas"), it was a common one in New Testament times. Not only were two of Jesus's disciples named Judas, but his half-brother was called Judas, too (Matthew 13:55). As a side note, the traditional teaching of the Catholic Church holds that Jesus's 'half-brothers' were actually his cousins, while the Protestant church views them as legitimate half-brothers. Jesus is also recorded to have had at least two half-sisters (Matthew 13:56).

Judas (in Greek) and *Judah* (in Hebrew) means 'praise' or 'God be praised or thanked'. Judas Iscariot's parents may have chosen the name in recognition of something significant—perhaps they were celebrating his conception or a safe delivery.

THE ROOT OF ALL KINDS OF EVIL

For reasons best known to Judas, he accepted money from the temple priests to betray Jesus's location (Luke 22:4-6, 52). Jesus was then arrested, tried, and executed by crucifixion. Despite this, Judas was, at least initially, very much part of the team of twelve disciples chosen by Jesus (Matthew 10:1). As Peter would later say, "He was one of our number and shared in this ministry" (Acts 1:17).

Within Judas lurked at least one major character flaw—the love of money. The Bible doesn't tell us what job Judas had before Jesus chose him as one of the twelve, but we do know that Matthew was a tax collector (Matthew 9:9). This would have made Matthew the more logical choice to be in charge of the finances, yet the job was given to Judas, despite him being a thief who stole from the group's funds (John 12:4-6).

We need to keep in mind that the love of money is the root of *all kinds* of evil (1 Timothy 6:10)—not the root of *all evil* as is often misquoted. Like most things, money is morally neutral and can be a means of achieving both good and evil outcomes.

Apart from money, two other reasons why Judas may have betrayed Jesus have been put forward. Firstly, Judas became disillusioned with Jesus and his spiritual mission, expecting instead that Jesus would overthrow the Roman occupiers. When it became clear that this wasn't going to happen, he betrayed him. Alternatively, he may have become convinced Jesus's actions were going to lead to a rebellion to try and overthrow the Romans (which Judas thought would end badly for his fellow Jews), and he betrayed Jesus to ensure such a revolt never occurred.

Few would probably choose to have Judas as a dinner guest, yet he would be able to tell us interesting things about Jesus, recount events that never made it into the Bible, and tell stories about the other eleven disciples.

FACING OUR FLAWS

We all possess character flaws. The trick is not to let them lead us into sin or negatively impact our relationship with Jesus. Judas may have betrayed Jesus to the authorities, but three times in a row Peter denied even knowing Jesus! Is one betrayal worse than a triple denial?

Peter managed to find a way back into a relationship with Jesus, and there has been debate as to whether Judas could have ever done likewise. Some have tried to claim the deck was stacked against Judas—that he had no choice and his actions were fated—but when he went to return the pieces of silver that he'd been paid for betraying Jesus, he said: "I have sinned . . . for I have betrayed innocent blood" (Matthew 27:4).

Judas chose not to make excuses for his sinful actions like, "I had no choice," or "the devil made me do it." Instead, he acknowledged and accepted his responsibility in the matter—and paid the price.

We should ask Jesus to help us sort out any character flaws *before* they lead us astray. Peter warns us what can happen when we follow our own sinful desires when he says, "people are slaves to whatever has mastered them" (2 Peter 2:19). Interestingly, some translations of that verse replace the word 'mastered' with 'bondage' or 'enslavement' instead.

There are many examples of people who have become enslaved by drugs, alcohol, pornography, gambling, or the search for recognition and affirmation on social media. They may start out thinking *they* are in control of the thing their flawed character has led them into. Yet, after a while, that thing begins to take over their life, and eventually, they no longer have control of it. Sin is progressive. The alcoholic didn't start out drinking a bottle of Vodka a day, nor did the gambling addict initially spend five hundred dollars per visit to the casino. It starts small, but soon you are constantly seeking more. Sin leads to enslavement; Jesus leads us to freedom. Let's choose wisely.

RETURN OF THE FISHERMAN

Nachman Koppelman
Harbour Master
Sea of Galilee

Simon Peter
The Fisherman's House
Capernaum

Date: A.D. 30

Dear Peter,

You're back! It must be, what, three years at least since you abandoned your fishing boat to follow Jesus on your quest to become a 'fisher of men'? I still have no idea what that was all about, but at least it turned out he wasn't a slave trader—my mistake. Don't be too sad things didn't work out. Becoming a 'fisher of men' was never going to lead to anything significant and certainly won't now that Jesus is dead. Anyway, it's fantastic you've returned to fishing.

A quick update since you left: Maria has added some really tasty goat burgers to her lunch bar menu. You really ought to try one—tell her you want it with cucumber sauce. With respect to moorings, it appears you have excellent timing as several have just become available—one quite close to Maria's Lunch Bar as it should so happen. Unfortunately, marina fees have increased in response to rising operating costs. Mooring rope alone has gone up by ten shekels a standard length, and oar prices are absolutely exorbitant. One would think they're making them out of pure gold these days. This brings me to the little matter of your unpaid mooring fees. Ring any bells? And, of course, someone—I'm not naming any names, but I think you know who—left their unwashed nets behind.

It was rather regrettable that Jesus got himself into trouble with the Roman authorities and ended up crucified. It's a nasty way to go, crucifixion, slow and painful. Is it true they put a crown of thorns[98] on his head? I'm also told they made him carry his own cross—well, at least as far as he could before they forced that Simon[99] guy to take over? Simon was a black dude from Cyrene in Africa, wasn't he? I saw it written somewhere, "Black African man carries the cross of a brown Jewish man sentenced to death by a white Roman man." These days, you don't see headlines like that as often as you used to.

Returning to fishing is a good choice, Peter. I just hope this time you plan to stick with it. I know Jesus talked about feeding people something called 'spiritual food'—whatever that is—but with fishing you're *really* feeding people, putting food in bellies and smiles on faces.

I'll have Maximus call round next week with a mooring agreement for you to sign. I'll put you down for site thirty-eight for the moment. It's near my office window—that way I can keep my eye on you to make sure you really are back fishing. If you behave yourself and stick with it, then next month I'll move you to mooring seventy-four, just down from the lunch bar.

In the meantime, please promise me you won't go rushing off to start some other venture like counting sheep, shearing sheep, or feeding sheep.[100] Sign up by the end of next week and I'll buy you and your brother Andrew a goat burger each. I'll even pay for cucumber sauce.

Yours,

Nachman Koppelman
Harbour Master

---

98 John 19:2
99 Mark 15:21
100 John 21:15-17

DISCUSSION

GOING 'BACK TO EGYPT'

Jesus chose twelve disciples to train up and continue his ministry. Yet when Jesus was crucified, the remaining eleven disciples (Judas having killed himself) became fearful and uncertain of what to do and hid themselves away. After a while, those who were fishermen returned to what they knew. Returning to something familiar when we feel lost or uncertain is a common response. It can provide us with emotional anchor points and even a level of comfort, but it doesn't necessarily mean it's always the right thing to do. Christians sometimes refer to this as 'going back to Egypt'.

After Moses led the Israelites out of slavery in Egypt, they soon found themselves in difficulty, trapped between the Red Sea and the advancing Egyptian army. At that point, some began to complain life would have been better *back in Egypt* (Exodus 14:10-12). They seemed to have forgotten they had, only recently, pleaded to God for help to escape their plight (Exodus 3:7).

How easy it is to only remember the good times and not the bad, to downplay in our mind how difficult a past situation was! We fool ourselves into thinking that 'the leopard will change its spots' and the unhealthy relationship we left behind will somehow be better if we return to it. We want to believe the other person

when they say they've changed (despite there being no proof they have) or claim 'things will be different this time'. Maybe we are trying to convince ourselves 'things will be different' if we go back to the way life was before. Sorry to say, but it doesn't work that way.

> *Neither can you do good who are accustomed to doing evil.*
>
> Jeremiah 13:23

SHEEP WITHOUT A SHEPHERD

Following Jesus's death, the chief priests and the Pharisees were worried that someone might steal Jesus's body, so they set a guard on his tomb (Matthew 27:62-65). Their worries were unfounded, as the disciples were, in fact, hiding inside a house behind a locked door (John 20:19-20). Stealing a dead body didn't feature anywhere on their 'to-do' list. Days later, Jesus appeared among them, implying he had either walked *through* the locked door, or his physical body had materialised in front of them. An impressive party trick either way!

We read that the disciples were hiding in a locked room but, according to John 21, they were also out fishing. Which one was it? Although they were initially fearful and hid in a locked room for days or even weeks, it appears they ventured out when it seemed safe to do so and returned to fishing and earning an income.

PETER IS RESTORED AND COMMISSIONED

Peter and at least six others were fishing on the Sea of Galilee when Jesus showed up on the shore, but they didn't recognise him. He told them to throw in their nets, and they caught an enormous quantity of fish (John 21:1-10). It was during this encounter that Jesus interacted with Peter, who, only a week or two earlier, had denied him three times in front of witnesses. Jesus restored him back into relationship with himself and commissioned him to feed his sheep—'sheep' being symbolic of Christian believers (John 21:15-17).

SIMON OF CYRENE

We meet Simon of Cyrene in three of the Gospels (Matthew 27:32; Mark 15:21; Luke 23:26). Cyrene was a town located in modern-day Libya, on the northern tip of Africa facing the Mediterranean Sea. As with many biblical figures, we are given little information about Simon. The Bible tells us all we *need* to know to find salvation and live the Christian life, but it often doesn't tell us everything we'd *like* to know (who *were* the wise men?). Although many people from Cyrene would have had black or dark skin, as far as Simon's skin colour is concerned, the Bible is silent. With Cyrene part of the globalised Roman empire, Simon could just as easily have been Greek or Italian, gentile or Jewish and had white or olive skin.

Jesus, covered in blood from being whipped and beaten, staggered under the weight of a heavy wooden cross as he headed towards Golgotha, or *Calvary* in Latin.

> *They brought Jesus to the place called Golgotha (which means "the place of the skull").*
>
> Mark 15:22

There would have been crowds watching as he passed by, some no doubt shouting insults. As Jesus weakened and carrying the cross became too much to bear, Simon of Cyrene was forced by the Romans to take over (Mark 15:21). How far he carried the cross, the Bible doesn't say.

CROWN OF THORNS

Jesus was made to wear a crown of thorns on the cross,[101] individual spikes which pierced his skull, painfully drawing blood. This is symbolic, as after sin entered the world through the actions of Adam and Eve, some plants began to grow thorns (Genesis 3:18). The thorns in Jesus's crown can, therefore, be viewed as a visual reminder and representation of humanity's sin.

THE SUFFERING OF THE INNOCENT

In the Book of Isaiah, there is a verse, considered by many to be prophetic, which vividly describes how Jesus would have appeared on the day of his crucifixion, quite

---

101 Matthew 27:27-29

different to how many crucifixion artworks depict him with only a few marks and cuts.

> *Many . . . were appalled at him—his appearance was so disfigured beyond that of any human being and his form marred beyond human likeness.*
>
> *Isaiah 52:14*

Such words conjure up an image of the worst and bloodiest crime scene—of a victim so savagely beaten they are scarcely recognisable for the person they once were, let alone recognisable as human. How much Jesus, the innocent, suffered for us, the guilty!

I SAY, IS THAT A TEAR IN THE CURTAIN?

Promised Land Curtains and Fabrics

Industrial Quarter

Jerusalem

Joseph Ben Caiaphas

The High Priest

Jerusalem Temple

Date: A.D. 30

Dear Caiaphas,

Last week, one of your over-enthusiastic temple guards burst into my office unannounced and immediately began shouting that the curtain in the temple had torn in two. I'm not a priest and do not go into the temple, so how should I know what state the thing is in?

"The High Priest says the matter is urgent," he shouted, moments before plunging a dagger into my desk. It was still covered in blood—his dagger, not my desk. Don't your guards take any pride in the appearance of their weapons these days? My desk is a rare six-hundred-year-old Egyptian antique—a copy of Pharaoh's own desk, in fact—and I don't appreciate your men leaving holes in it.

Yes, we supplied the curtain a long time ago, but it was your priests who installed it. It was manufactured to the highest possible quality, and many thousands of snails gave up their lives to make the required purple dye.[102] Since your man visited, we've

---

102   Exodus 26:31-33. Its rare purple colour was obtained from a dye made using a particular species of snail called the Murex.

performed tests on the curtain's linen yarn, which still can't explain how the damage occurred, although it is clear it was not cut, but torn, from top to bottom.

As you know, given the curtain's size[103] and weight it would be challenging for anyone— even if they possessed the strength of Samson—to inflict such damage on it. Speaking of, have you checked the damage isn't an act of revenge by some distant descendant of the Philistines? I seem to recall they weren't very happy with blind old Samson right at the end there. Didn't he leave the temple of their god Dagon in a pile of rubble and kill a few thousand Dagon worshippers in the process?[104] I'd also be tempted to suggest a descendant of Goliath's family may be responsible, but even he only topped out at three metres—a little on the short side for a curtain almost twenty metres high. You haven't had it dry-cleaned recently, have you? I had a sports jacket dry-cleaned the other day, and afterwards, one of the arms tore right off. They just aren't careful, these dry cleaners, despite what they claim. Especially that store, Jacob's Dry Cleaning— Coloured coats a speciality.

Your Mr 'Stab-a-Desk' mentioned that agitator Jesus, and I know you and him weren't best buddies. However, he had succumbed to death by crucifixion moments before the curtain was torn,[105] so he probably isn't your man. Have you considered a disgruntled member of the Sanhedrin could be responsible instead? The word on the street is that a Pharisee named Nicodemus has jumped the fence and joined the Jesus mob, too. Then again, maybe the man you seek is Peter—a Jesus follower. He left Jesus's trial early and vanished into the night[106] to . . . tear the temple curtain perhaps? If it was him, you will let me know how he did it, won't you, High Priest? It's just professional curiosity on my part, of course, and could help us design rip-proof curtains in the future.

Finally, and this is just a thought from 'left field' as they say, is it at all possible God was using the torn curtain to send those of you at the temple a message like, "It's all over chaps, time to find a new job?" Weird sort of messaging system, I know, but surely

---

103   Its size was approximately sixty feet high by thirty feet wide.

104   Judges 16:23-30

105   Matthew 27:51

106   Matthew 26:69-75

it's worth considering given the lack of other plausible explanations. I recall Jesus mentioning something about the temple being destroyed.[107] Perhaps he arranged for someone to start with the curtain, and one day the whole thing will be nothing more than a pile of rubble. Like that would ever happen!

High Priest, we both know curtains don't tear by themselves, just as Egyptian antique desks don't repair themselves. Consequently, I've attached a quote for the cost to repair the curtain and a second quote which covers the damage to my desk. It turns out the desk will have to be shipped back to Egypt to get fitted with replacement parts that aren't available in Jerusalem. The lingering blood stains left by your man's dagger also need some attention. Perhaps next time he comes you could tell him to knock on my office door first, you know, like normal people do.

Yours sincerely,

Bartholomew Jedidiah
Manager

---

107 Matthew 24:2 When Jesus speaks of the destruction of the 'temple', he is referring to his own body.

DISCUSSION

A NEW SYSTEM

The tearing of the temple curtain signalled the changeover from the Old Covenant, with its system of sacrificing animals, to the New Covenant, where sin was dealt with through the eternal sacrifice of Jesus. Fundamentally, the curtain represented a separation between man and God. Animal sacrifices made on behalf of people were handled by priests, and once a year a national sacrifice was made by the High Priest on The Day of Atonement or *Yom Kippur*. Blood from this sacrifice was sprinkled inside the Holy of Holies at the heart of the Jewish temple.

High priests could only come from the tribe of Levi and had to be descendants of Aaron, the brother of Moses. Other Levites not descended from Aaron fulfilled the other temple duties. It was a system that had operated since the Israelites entered the desert with Moses, where an animal's shed blood was used to atone for the guilty.

> *For the life of a creature is in the blood, and I have given it to you to make atonement for yourselves on the altar; it is the blood that makes atonement for one's life.*
>
> *Leviticus 17:11*

However, there remained a fundamental problem. It didn't matter how many animals were sacrificed, animal blood simply couldn't take away sin.

> *But those sacrifices are an annual reminder of sins. It is impossible for the blood of bulls and goats to take away sins.*
>
> *Hebrews 10:3-4*

While the separation between God and man remained, the curtain was staying put. What was needed was a *permanent* sin solution, but how? When John the Baptist saw Jesus approaching, he said: "Look, the Lamb of God, who takes away the sin of the world!" (John 1:29). Jesus would one day sacrifice himself in our place and carry our sin. As a result, through our faith in Jesus, we gain right standing—righteousness—with God the Father.

> *God made [Jesus] who had no sin to be sin for us, so that in him we might become the righteousness of God.*
>
> *2 Corinthians 5:21*

OUR GREAT HIGH PRIEST

Even if Jesus could be sacrificed in our place as a 'sacrificial lamb', there remained obstacles to him completing the ceremony. Firstly, only those from the tribe of Levi could become priests and enter the temple, and, secondly, only the High Priest could enter past the curtain to sprinkle the blood. Jesus wasn't from the tribe of Levi (his tribe was Judah), and he wasn't a high priest. Yet something had to be done. In Hebrews 7:11, we read that even the Levitical priesthood with its sacrificial offerings couldn't bring perfection to humanity, and neither could the law upon which those sacrifices were based.

Game over for God? Not quite. God always has a plan even if we can't see it. And on this occasion, no one saw the plan. If they had, they would never have allowed Jesus anywhere near the cross.

> *None of the rulers of this age understood it, for if they had, they would not have crucified the Lord of glory.*
> *1 Corinthians 2:8*

Actually, Jesus *is* our High Priest. *He is? I thought you said he wasn't from the tribe of Levi?* He wasn't. He was appointed to the position of High Priest by God—not from the Levitical priesthood but from the order of Melchizedek.

Consider for a moment the honours system used in Commonwealth countries. Most recipients are nominated for an honour by certain organisations, government departments, or by the public before being approved by a committee. However, there are several awards (for example the Order of the Thistle) that are conferred at the personal discretion of the sovereign of the United Kingdom. Similarly, whereas the Levitical priesthood more or less followed an automatic committee-approval system, the Melchizedek priesthood was offered at God's personal discretion.

Even as a Melchizedek-type high priest (Hebrews 6:20, 7:17; Psalm 110:4), Jesus did not enter the Holy of Holies in the Jerusalem Temple (you still had to be a Levite high priest to do that). Rather, Jesus entered the original Holy of Holies, located in heaven and upon which the one on earth was based (Hebrews 8:5). There, he made one perfect sacrifice, valid forever.

> *When Christ came as high priest of the good things that are now already here, he went through the greater and more perfect tabernacle that is not made with human hands, that is to say, not a part of this creation. He did not enter by means of the blood of goats and calves; but he entered the Most Holy Place once for all by his own blood, thus obtaining eternal redemption.*
> *Hebrews 9:11-12*

With Jesus's perfect sacrifice finally resolving the sin problem once and for all, the earthly system was no longer required. The old covenant and its sacrifices, priests, much of its law and temple had come to an end, and the New Covenant Jesus spoke of (Matthew 26:27-28) was now in effect. God signalled this transition with the tearing of the curtain—not unlike tearing up the sheets of a contract that has just become void.

> *Nor did he enter heaven to offer himself again and again, the way the high priest enters the Most Holy Place every year with blood that is not his own. Then Christ would have had to suffer many times since the creation of the world. But he has appeared once for all at the end of the*

ages to do away with sin by the sacrifice of himself.

Hebrews 9:25-26

DESTRUCTION OF THE EARTHLY TEMPLE

In A.D. 70, the Romans, quelling a Jewish revolt, destroyed the temple, and it has never been rebuilt since. Instead, God now invites us directly into his presence.

Therefore, brothers and sisters, since we have confidence to enter the Most Holy Place by the blood of Jesus, by a new and living way opened for us through the curtain, that is, his body . . .

Hebrews 10:19-20

Furthermore, what was once for Jewish people only has now been expanded to include Jews and gentiles alike.

Remember that at that time you were separate from Christ, excluded from citizenship in Israel and foreigners to the covenants of the promise, without hope and without God in the world. But now in Christ Jesus you who once were far away have been brought near by the blood of Christ.

Ephesians 2:12-13

In one day, Jesus achieved for humanity what well over one thousand years of Levite priests and a multitude of sacrificed animals could not.

A CAT AND DOG
(AND MR T)

Psychological Services Ltd

Mental Health Hub

Gadarene Avenue

Jerusalem

Calixtus Placida Fedelis

Chief of Staff

Fort Antonia

Jerusalem

Date: A.D. 30

Re: Mental State of Soldier Cassius Longinus[108]

Dear Calixtus,

Concerned over rising mental health issues among its soldiers, the Roman army decided several years ago to launch a new wellness programme. It provides soldiers with access to CAT (Counselling and Therapy) and DOG (Developmental Occupational Guidance). Additionally, soldiers must meet MR T (Mentally Required Toughness) in order to be deemed fit for service.[109] Psychological Services Ltd are contracted by the army to provide a specialised counselling service referred to as FAT-CAT (First

---

108 The soldier who speared Jesus's side (John 19:34) is unnamed in the Bible but is historically believed by many to have been Longinus. His spear is variously referred to as 'The Spear of Destiny' or 'The Holy Lance'. It features in the 2023 movie, *Indiana Jones and the Dial of Destiny* where it is referred to as the 'Lance of Longinus'.

109 Mr T is an American actor who played the role of B. A. Baracus in the 1980s television action-adventure show, *The A-Team*.

Aid Through Counselling and Therapy). Usually, interactions between our staff and a soldier remain confidential but a recent situation concerning Legionnaire Longinus now requires disclosure (as per section LX.XV.II of the contract's privacy provisions).

During one of his counselling sessions, Longinus told me that following the crucifixion of Jesus of Nazareth, he was the soldier who thrust a spear into his side to ensure he was truly dead. Longinus's problems started three days later after hearing stories claiming Jesus was no longer dead. He also admits to interacting with several of Jesus's followers. These stories began messing with his head, and he applied under WOOF (Welfare Of Official Fighters) to get some CAT and a spot of DOG. He now thinks anyone he kills might return to life to take revenge on him.

You and I, Calixtus, both know that dead people stay dead—that's the way it's been for centuries—yet Longinus has become convinced otherwise. I've tried my best to help him understand that he is experiencing a delusion—one that will pass, given time. I've pointed out that Jesus's resurrection from the dead isn't real and is just a story made up by his grieving followers. Then Longinus claimed he'd seen, with his own eyes, Jesus walking the streets of Jerusalem. In addition to believing the dead can live again, he's now begun seeing them.

I've dived into my therapeutic bag of tools as deeply as I can in my quest to help him, but his is one of the most stubborn cases I've ever encountered. I've tried diversion therapy (after initial success, he diverted *back* to believing Jesus is alive), narrative therapy (he kept saying Jesus was alive), and art therapy (he drew a picture of an empty tomb with the caption: "Jesus has risen"). Music therapy was no better—he spent the entire session singing, "Up from the grave he arose."[110] Drama therapy began positively, with him lying on the floor of my office not moving for thirty minutes, repeating, "Jesus is dead". However, just as the session was finishing and I thought we'd made a real breakthrough, he jumped up shouting, "Jesus is alive, he's risen again!"

In desperation, as I personally don't like large animals, I obtained a horse, thinking we could try equine therapy. A pile of horse dung and a lingering smell later, Longinus responded by claiming Jesus would return one day, riding a white horse. I now

110   The title of a hymn written and composed in 1874 by Robert Lowry (1826-1899).

consider his case to be beyond help. I can only recommend dismissing him from the army under the provisions of DIMWIT (Dismiss Immediately, Mentally Wounded by Ingrained Trauma). I'm afraid no amount of CAT or DOG is ever going to produce MR T in Longinus.

Yours,

Turibius Viator
Chief Therapist

DISCUSSION

HISTORICAL EVIDENCE FOR THE CRUCIFIXION

Possibly invented by the Persians between 300-400 B.C., crucifixion is said to be one of the most painful ways to die. The Romans carried out this brutal form of execution for many years before it was used on Jesus. They continued it until sometime in the fourth century when it was banned under Emperor Constantine, who was said to have converted to Christianity in A.D. 312.

Evidence of crucifixion being carried out elsewhere in the world has resurfaced from time to time, including in Nagasaki, Japan in 1597 where a group of twenty-six foreign Catholic priests and local laymen were put to death by crucifixion on the orders of Japan's ruler, Toyotomi Hideyoshi.[111] Today, in Nagasaki, you will find a memorial to the twenty-six, alongside a museum devoted to telling the story of their lives and the development of Christianity in Japan. In terms of its population size, Tokyo is the largest city in Japan, while Nagasaki is a distant thirty-fifth. Yet when we look at ranking lists of the number of Christians per population size, Nagasaki is second only to Tokyo.[112] Did the deaths of those priests and local laymen all

those years ago somehow allow the gospel to bear more fruit in the city? The numbers would suggest so.

Although it is clearly detailed in biblical accounts, there was, until recently, a distinct lack of archaeological evidence to support crucifixion in and around Israel. However, in 1968, an ossuary—a container holding the bones of the dead—was discovered a short distance north of Jerusalem which contained a heel bone with an iron nail driven through it. Many view this as physical evidence confirming the biblical accounts of crucifixions.

JESUS'S DEATH AND BURIAL

Sometimes, crucified bodies were left by the Romans to rot as a warning to others, but not so the body of Jesus. In accordance with the law (Deuteronomy 21:23), Jewish leaders didn't want bodies to be on display during the Sabbath. To prevent this from happening, those who were being crucified—in this case, Jesus and two criminals—were to have their legs broken to speed up death (John 19:31-33). This was not necessary for Jesus as he was already dead, but just to be certain, a Roman soldier plunged a spear into his side.

A man called Joseph of Arimathea requested the body of Jesus from Pilate. Pilate was the Roman governor of the Judea region and had been reluctant to have Jesus crucified to begin

---

111 https://en.wikipedia.org/wiki/26_Martyrs_of_Japan

112 Proportion of Christians in Japanese cities www.nippon.com/en/features/h00200

with. Even his wife had warned him against getting involved (Matthew 27:19-24). Eventually, Pilate washed his hands of the matter which may explain why he let Joseph take the body away for burial so quickly.

Nicodemus, a Pharisee who had previously met with Jesus at night to discuss religious matters (John 3:1-14), helped Joseph with the burial. It would appear Nicodemus had come to believe in Jesus, although this is not stated explicitly in the Bible. It offers a good explanation, however, for why a Pharisee would allow himself to become ceremonially unclean by helping to bury the body of a man many of the other Pharisees hated.

A CULTURAL CONVERSION

Converting to Christianity doesn't require that people surrender their distinct cultural or ethnic identity—although once you do become a Christian, others in the group might subsequently reject you. However, like Nicodemus, a person does need to give up any cultural or group practices that go against the teachings of the Bible. Early missionaries, for example, had to teach converts from some jungle tribes that revenge killings and cannibalism weren't permitted. In Europe, missionaries had to instruct new converts to give up their occult and divination practices. Furthermore, every convert to Jesus must give up belief in any other god. The moral portion of the Old Testament Law, which is still in force, says, "You shall have no other gods before me" (Exodus 20:3). What this really means is having *no other gods at all*.

For Jewish converts (such as Nicodemus), the God of Moses, Abraham, and Isaac whom they worship is also the God of the Christian. However, when presented with the knowledge of Jesus—a more complete revelation of God to humanity and the bringer of a new covenant— they must (as must everyone) choose to place their faith in him for their salvation (Acts 4:11-12). Any Jew or gentile who worships God according to their current understanding and is subsequently presented with the gospel message, must accept Jesus as their saviour to obtain salvation under the New Covenant.

A GLOBAL RELIGION

Many have claimed that Christianity is a 'white man's religion'. Coming from the Middle East, Jesus and his followers most likely had brown or olive-coloured skin. They certainly would not have had pale white skin. Skin colour shouldn't be the detail that validates a belief system. That said, as Christianity originated in the Middle East, it has never been a 'European religion' nor a 'white man's religion' at its origin.

In Acts 8:26-38 we read of the first convert from Africa—a eunuch from Ethiopia. It isn't until eight chapters later, in Acts 16:13-16, that we come across the first Christian convert in Europe—a woman named Lydia. So, from a biblical perspective, Christianity arrived in Africa before it reached Europe. Furthermore, the Bible was translated into Ge'ez, an ancient language of Ethiopia, sometime between A.D. 500-700 making it many centuries older than the first English version of 1535 (or the King James Version of 1611).[113]

It's important to remember that Christianity has always been a religion for all, no matter their language, ethnic background or skin colour. In the words of Galatians 3:28, "There is neither Jew nor Gentile, neither slave nor free, nor is there male and female, for you are all one in Christ Jesus."

---

113 John Wycliffe produced an English version around A.D. 1384, but translated it from an existing Latin version. William Tyndale's bible of 1535 was translated directly from Hebrew and Greek texts.

PETER'S REPUTATION REHABILITATION

Reputation Rehabilitation Services
Level 5, The Tiberius Tower
Capernaum

Peter the Apostle
Fisherman's House
Sea of Galilee
Capernaum

Date: A.D. 30

Dear Peter,

I understand you have expressed concerns that some of your behaviour on the night of Jesus's trial may have negatively affected your reputation. That night, you promised Jesus that, "Even if all fall away on account of you, I never will."[114] Jesus had tried telling you that before the night was over and the rooster had crowed you would deny him three times. Despite this warning—or perhaps you just weren't listening—you boasted all the more, saying, and I quote, "Even if I have to die with you, I will never disown you."[115]

Brave words indeed, but the follow-through was lacking. By the time you reached the third denial, you were calling down curses and swearing that you didn't even know the man![116] You spent three years with Jesus, and this was the best you could come up with? Perhaps the less said, the better.

---

114   Matthew 26:33
115   Matthew 26:35
116   Matthew 26:74

Usually, the first step we'd take in sorting out this type of mess would be to issue a press release redirecting blame. It might state that you were misquoted or misheard, your statements referred to someone else, or your words were taken out of context. For example, we could claim the full version of what you said was: "I don't know the man you think Jesus is, but he's my best friend!" Another approach would be to redirect the blame for your outburst onto something else—such as suffering from elevated levels of stress. Far more convincing would be to say you had an ember in your eye from the fire[117] causing you to mistake Jesus for another person, and that when you said you didn't 'know the man', you were referring to someone you thought was a Roman centurion. By the way, do you recall seeing any Roman centurions on duty that night? It would help with credibility if there were some present.

Another possible approach is to re-direct attention away from your faux pas by focusing on your good deeds and contributions to society. We can subsequently demonstrate that the behaviour in question was an out-of-character slip-up and not the 'real you'. So, what have you done to help society? Have you given away donations of fish to the poor, undertaken fundraising for widows, or helped out on a working bee at the temple? Ever run a 'teach a child to fish' programme, or given free boat rides during Passover celebrations?

Peter, any statement made about you has to be believable. Asking around, I find you've previously made some rather wild claims in the past, including walking on water and seeing Moses and Elijah talking with Jesus up a mountain.[118] I'm wondering if you missed the memo on that last one—Moses and Elijah are both dead. Then again, maybe you really did see them. After all, when it comes to Moses, we are only assuming he's dead, given that no one can find his grave. He would certainly be getting on a bit . . . how long has it been now, sixteen hundred years? As far as Elijah is concerned, the temple scrolls say he was taken up into the sky in a flying chariot—a little too quickly it would seem, as he dropped his cloak on departure. Fortunately, some chap called Elisha who was standing nearby was good enough to pick it up and give it a wash in

---

117 John 18:18
118 Matthew 17:1-4

the nearby Jordan River.[119] So, maybe Elijah isn't dead either.

Anyhow, as I said, it's all about credibility, and some of your claims definitely lack the level of credibility we require. I think the best thing for you to do would be to lie low until things blow over. Definitely don't go involving yourself with anything to do with real estate. The last thing we want is for you to get yourself tied up in a property sale that results in a pile of dead bodies.

Finally, I hear that you've been attending meetings in the Upper Room[120] where over one hundred of you wait expectantly for something to happen. You need to let it go. Jesus is gone. All you're doing now is having the largest shared lunch in history. You say Jesus is going to return—well, why not do your own 'return' while you are waiting? Go back to fishing. They say you went back to fishing once before, and some things are easier to do the second time around. I also hear there's a particularly good lunch bar at the marina.

Yours,

Zechariah Cantor
Senior PR Advisor

---

119   2 Kings 2:11-14
120   Acts 1:12-15

DISCUSSION

PETER'S BOLD CLAIMS

Jesus and eleven of the disciples (Judas having left while they were eating) finished their Passover meal and began walking to the Mount of Olives. During a discussion that evening, Peter boldly claimed he would stand with Jesus regardless of what might happen.

"Even if I have to die with you, I will never disown you" (Matthew 26:35). Not only did Peter make the claim, but all the other disciples said the same (Matthew 26:35).

Afterwards, Jesus wandered off to pray, and when he returned he told Peter that he also should pray:

> "Watch and pray so that you will not fall into temptation. The spirit is willing, but the flesh is weak."
>
> *Matthew 26:41*

JESUS ARRESTED

Peter didn't follow Jesus's advice, and when Judas appeared with an armed mob to arrest Jesus, instead of *rock, paper, scissors*, Peter played *sword, ear, blood* with the servant of the High Priest. The servant lost both the game and his ear (John 18:10) and Peter was told by Jesus to put his sword away. Should

Jesus require help, he could call on the twelve legions[121] of angels the Father had standing by. Yet Jesus allowed himself to be arrested, and the disciples fled (Matthew 26:56). One could argue that the other disciples—who had also sworn never to disown Jesus—also denied him in that moment by their act of fleeing. Peter was the exception, following Jesus to the place where he was put on trial (Matthew 26:58).

UNDER PRESSURE

As Peter sat watching the trial, a servant girl began asking him difficult questions and accusing him of being connected with Jesus. Peter denied it. When the accusations kept coming, he made another denial. After his third denial (Matthew 26:74) Peter left the area, weeping bitterly, having not lived up to the bold promises he'd earlier made to Jesus.

How do we respond when confronted with the challenge to acknowledge Jesus? If we deny Jesus in some situation of our own, are we any less guilty than Peter?

DID PETER LOSE HIS SALVATION WHEN HE DENIED CHRIST?

Was it three strikes and you're out for Peter (and is it for us)? It is clear that Peter badly stumbled and faltered at the very moment when he could have stood with Christ. It is also clear that fear of persecution and the desire for self-preservation played a significant part in

---

121 At full strength, a legion of Roman soldiers numbered 6000 men (12 x 6000 = 72,000 angels).

his actions, as indeed they might in our own if we were faced with something similar. Maybe you haven't denied Christ—instead, perhaps a particular sin has got hold of your heart and you are wondering if you've done something so bad Jesus won't forgive you. Maybe you even wonder if you've lost your salvation?

Will Jesus reject you because of what you've done or become involved with? Drugs you took to control pain have turned into an addiction. You blasphemed in a stressful moment or loneliness led you deeper and deeper into pornography. The devil will happily tell you that Jesus is revolted by your actions, that he disowns you, that you have lost your salvation. Instead, Jesus responds with, "I took it all to the cross, I forgive you, keep going and try again."

It is said that dementia is serious, not so much when a person can't remember that an item is called a can opener, but when they can't remember what a can opener is used for. Likewise, it is not that we have sinned again (unhelpful as that is), but if having done so, we no longer care that we have, or feel any remorse for doing so. Peter cared about what he'd done and felt plenty of remorse.

OBSERVATIONS

Jesus predicted Peter would fail, and warned him to pray (advice not taken). God knows we too might fail in some way due to fear, or finding ourselves in a pressure cooker situation. He understands our response when we find our life, well-being, or freedom at risk. God knows and understands our motives and weaknesses.

After denying Christ, Peter realised the magnitude of what he had done and experienced profound grief and remorse (Matthew 26:75). We get a hint that God was very aware of how Peter was feeling from this verse:

> *But go, tell his disciples and Peter, "He is going ahead of you into Galilee. There you will see him, just as he told you."*
>
> *Mark 16:7*

These words were spoken by an angel to the women who had turned up to Jesus's tomb only to find it empty. They were told to specifically make sure they told Peter that Jesus was alive again and where he could find him.

Some say that because Peter didn't acknowledge Jesus in the situation, he lost his salvation. They base this claim on the following scripture:

> *Whoever acknowledges me before others, I will also acknowledge before my Father in heaven. But whoever disowns me before others, I will disown before my Father in heaven.*
>
> *Matthew 10:32-33*

Yes, Peter had failed to acknowledge Jesus, but did so in a specific and one-off situation—none of us perform perfectly on all occasions. I do not believe he lost his salvation, as he was genuinely remorseful over his denials of Jesus. Had he continued to deny Jesus and abandon his faith, then there would be grounds to question his salvation. But he didn't do that.

JESUS RESPONDS

If Peter had lost his salvation for failing at a time of extreme stress, what hope would there be for the rest of us? But Jesus never abandoned Peter, and if we remain genuine in heart, regardless of how we might feel, he won't abandon us. Instead, when the disciples met up with Jesus again, Jesus cooked breakfast for Peter and the other disciples. When the dishes were done, he spoke directly with Peter and restored their relationship (John 21).

Peter went on to become the leader of the church in Jerusalem, and years later, Paul visited and stayed with him for fifteen days (Galatians 1:18). These are not the outcomes of a man who has lost his salvation. Even in our darkest moments, even when our behaviour may be at its worst, God's river of grace and forgiveness runs wide and deep.

If we confess our sins, he is faithful and just and will forgive us our sins and purify us from all unrighteousness.

1 John 1:9

A JURISPRUDENCE NIGHTMARE

Cohen, Stern & Steinbach

Lawyers, Accountants and Business Advisers

3rd Floor, Jerusalem Plaza

Laurentius Lucius

Attorney General

Department of Jurisprudence & Courts

Stone Tablets Quarter

Jerusalem

Date: A.D. 30

Dear Laurentius,

Allow me to recap recent events. Less than two weeks ago, Jesus of Nazareth was crucified—and that's when the weird stuff started happening. Firstly, the giant curtain hanging inside the temple was mysteriously torn in half. To be fair, it *was* rather old, but the repair bill is truly eyewatering. It certainly made the High Priest's eyes water! More significantly, a sizeable earthquake struck at around the same time, and people who were once dead and buried suddenly came alive and began crawling out of their tombs.[122] The first thing that became obvious was the quantity and quality of grave clothes some undertakers had used. One chap had only been wrapped in a thin layer of material and you could see . . . never mind.

---

122   Matthew 27:51-53

Newspaper headlines such as: "Honey, I'm home from the grave!" and "Dead? I'm not dead!" haven't been helping matters. I've just finished organising witness protection for a client who, before they died, gave a testimony that helped put someone away. Upon hearing my client is alive again, that previously incarcerated individual is now on the hunt for revenge. It was the case involving the centurion, the pharisee who got drunk at the Duck and Feather, and a Prefect's daughter who suffered from an uncontrollable urge to . . . never mind.

If these people are considered legally 'undead', are they now automatically considered re-married to any spouses they had before their deaths? More importantly, what's the situation if the 'dead' person's previous husband or wife has since remarried? Several people I've spoken to are rather worried about this. For example, a woman could suddenly find herself married to both her original 'dead' husband *and* her current husband. Their concern is that someone at the temple might view this as adultery and order all three of them to be stoned. I know it sounds over the top, but Jesus regularly accused these religious teachers of being extreme, saying they were guilty of straining at a gnat and eating a camel afterwards.[123] (I didn't get the thing about eating camels either—probably something to do with their special religious diet.) Fortunately, everyone at the temple is currently rather preoccupied with raising money to pay for the curtain repair.

I've just finished organising bail for a very upset husband. Alive again, he arrived home and walked in on his 'wife' showing affection to her new husband. She tried explaining the situation, but the deceased first husband didn't believe a word of it. The police were called, and he ended up spending time in the cells to cool off. He shouted it wasn't legal to jail dead people, and he has a fair point. On paper he's still dead, so *is* it legal to put him in the cells? Doing so might leave the police open to a charge of grave-robbing, while pressing charges against the husband would technically involve prosecuting a corpse.

I'm concerned we are heading into uncharted waters, legally speaking. Another case I'm dealing with involves a woman who was married to Magnus Abrams. She died,

---

123 Matthew 23:24

and sometime later Magnus remarried. Recently, Magnus also died and left behind his second wife. However, before his estate could be settled, the earthquake occurred and his first wife came back to life. In his will, Magnus had written, "I leave everything to my wife," without naming her. Both wives appeared in my office yesterday, each claiming they were the sole beneficiary of Magnus's will. Does the first wife's return to life cancel the provisions of his will, or should I divide his estate and give them half each? Existing law seems unclear on this matter. Now that his original wife is alive again, it could be argued that his first marriage remains in effect. His marriage to the second wife could then be seen to constitute polygamy and, as that is illegal, this would exclude her from inheriting his estate.

Yesterday, one of the undead turned up and freaked out an office lady so badly she had to take the afternoon off. She's the one I told you about who got drunk at that wedding in Cana three years ago when all the free wine suddenly appeared out of nowhere. She got herself so drunk she wasn't able to return to work for days.

Anyway, it's certainly been a hectic day so far. There's a criminal case I need to sort out involving a man sentenced to five years in jail but who died two years into the sentence. His lawyer is asking my legal opinion as to whether his client must serve the remaining three years, now he is alive again.

Another case involves a man who purchased a 'lifetime' taxi pass. Under the 'continuity of contract' clause, the company refused to accept it because he'd died and was no longer able to continue using the service. As a result, they say they are no longer obligated to keep providing him free rides, and he needs to buy a new pass. As you can see, these certainly are unprecedented times!

Yours,

Arron Cohen
Cohen, Stern & Steinbach

DISCUSSION

MYSTERIES OF THE RESURRECTION

A number of seemingly inexplicable events took place when Jesus died. For three hours while he was on the cross, the midday sky turned dark. As he breathed his last, the temple curtain was torn from top to bottom. Soon thereafter, an earthquake struck, and a group of dead people came back to life.

Bible scholars have long wondered, debated and speculated about who these newly resurrected people were—the Bible calls them saints or holy people—and what their appearing meant. It is unclear whether they continued living on earth or returned to heaven with Jesus forty days after his resurrection. We may just need to mark this one down as another fascinating biblical mystery that won't be fully understood until we get to heaven.

MYSTERIES OF THE BIBLE

The Bible contains various passages that can be difficult to interpret, or even figure out what's going on. For example, 1 Timothy 2:15 says that women will be saved through childbearing. Does this mean a woman must give birth in order to be saved? Is a woman's salvation dependent on her continuing to have babies and, if so, how many? What if a woman isn't fertile?

Things become clearer and less complicated if we look at this passage through a different lens. When Paul was writing to Timothy, he was *not saying* women had to have babies to achieve salvation, rather that if they were not able to gather with the church because of their maternal responsibilities, their salvation was still secure.

Sometimes, things aren't intended to be taken literally. For example, in John 10:9 when Jesus says: "I am the gate," he isn't saying he is a physical gate with a handle and hinges. When we read passages like Matthew 5:30, which refers to cutting off one's hand to avoid sin, it doesn't mean we should do it literally. Rather, it is an example of *hyperbole*—exaggeration for effect. Jesus used such language to drive home the seriousness of sin and its consequences.

People sometimes deliberately misquote or use verses out of context. Sometimes, in order to support a particular teaching or belief, they only quote part of a verse[124] because quoting it in full would quickly lead to a different understanding of the matter. An extreme example of this would be to declare that the Bible says, "There is no God." However, if you read the whole verse, it says: "The fool says in his heart, 'There is no God'" (Psalm 14:1). So, the Bible doesn't say

---

124 Throughout this book, I have occasionally quoted part of a verse. This is only to save space or because the remainder of it relates to a different topic. This is why I encourage people to read the full verse in a Bible and then come to their own conclusion on the matter.

there is no God, rather that only foolish people make that claim.

In order to determine the meaning of more difficult passages, we first need to read them in context. This means looking at the verses which precede and follow it. When it comes to the Gospels, some stories are repeated across several of them and, in a few cases, the stories appear in all four. Often, each account will provide a few details the others don't include, and by combining *all the details*, we are able to assemble a clearer picture of what's happening. Over the years, many Bible commentaries (most now freely available online) have been written in which scholars offer their views and unpack the meaning of a given passage of Scripture. Helpful as these commentaries are, one should also pray to God for greater understanding of his Word.

Occasionally, no consensus can be found on the meaning or best interpretation of a passage of Scripture. Uncertainty can often arise in the Old Testament, as it isn't always clear how a specific Hebrew word should be translated. Similar challenges occur when translating the (now unused) early Greek language used to write the New Testament. (The wider use of *koine* Greek, or biblical Greek, ended by the fifth century A.D., eventually being replaced by modern Greek.)

Still, we shouldn't be discouraged. If we attend a church whose leaders believe the Bible to be the inspired Word of God and consistently preach from it, we will ultimately develop a better understanding of Scripture, no matter how mysterious it might seem.

THINGS TURN DEADLY IN REAL ESTATE

Community Development Group
Old City Chambers
Jerusalem

Andrew the Apostle
The Way HQ
Jerusalem

Date: A.D. 30

Dear Andrew,

Today I learnt that a local couple, Ananias and Sapphira, dropped dead during a religious meeting conducted by your brother, Peter. I accept that on the odd occasion people die during religious meetings. It's unpleasant but it happens. What I don't accept is that two healthy individuals attending the same service died within hours of one another. That, Andrew, is more than a little suspicious. What's even more suspicious is the fact that both died immediately after talking to Peter.

With no autopsy performed, how are we to know whether they died from natural causes or suspicious ones? Despite my best efforts, I haven't been able to discover who signed the death certificate verifying them as officially dead. I'm not suggesting they were buried alive, at least not deliberately. However, mistakes do happen, and without a death certificate, well, Peter can't prove they really were dead, can he now? Entombed alive while attending a religious gathering isn't the sort of headline the city wants to see.

I also have to question Peter's methods. One day he's preaching on salvation, trying to grow the movement's numbers, the next he's holding a religious service that finishes with fewer people alive than when it started. That's just crazy. Continue like that and it won't be long before your movement becomes extinct. Let's be honest, who wants to attend a religious meeting knowing that it could be their last? Certainly not me. Furthermore, dead bodies piling up at the feet of a preacher is hardly what you would call 'seeker friendly' now, is it? Worse still if it should happen during a healing meeting! At this rate, an Alpha service could quickly turn into an Omega[125] one. Instead of passing out visitor cards, Peter may want to consider distributing 'make your own will' kits.

If I've been informed correctly, Ananias placed a pile of money at Peter's feet.[126] Peter asked him, "Is that all of it?"[127] and Ananias replied, "Sure thing, dude." Peter paused before responding; "Liar, liar, pants on fire," and Ananias dropped dead. At least Peter arranged to have his corpse removed and buried. His wife, Sapphira, soon made an appearance, and rather than telling her that her husband was dead, Peter grilled her on the sale price of some property the pair had sold. After hearing her out, Peter said, "What a load of baloney," and she too dropped dead and was buried. By the way, I'd like to know who is paying for all these graveyard plots? Your religion and real estate clearly don't mix. Are you aware that after word got out about what happened, house sales were down thirty-seven percent in the region for the month?

Are house sales your movement's version of a temple tax? If so, it's a jolly expensive one. Perhaps it's not a tax at all but a multilevel marketing scheme with Peter sitting at the top of Ananias and Sapphira's up-line. Unhappy with their performance, he decided to cut them out and take control of all of their down-lines. I could be wrong—perhaps it's a Ponzi scheme[128] or a pyramid scheme, or Peter just scheming in general.

---

125 *Alpha (α)* is the first letter of the Greek alphabet, *Omega (Ω)* the last. 'Alpha' is also a special programme churches run to introduce Christianity to non-Christians. www.alpha.org/home/

126 Acts 5:2 The money was delivered to 'all the apostles', not just Peter.

127 The actual conversation is recorded in Acts 5:1-11.

128 A fraudulent financial 'investment' that effectively robs Peter to pay Paul. Named after Charles Ponzi who ran one during the 1920s.

A number of people who attended the service approached me afterwards saying how frightened they were. "Scariest religious meeting I've attended in my life," one said. Another commented, "This new Jesus thing is not for me, I'm going back to the temple." Whatever happened, it definitely isn't a good look for the city. I'm quite disappointed in Peter's actions and feel Jerusalem would be better off, and far safer, if he went back fishing.

Yours,

Josiah Ben-Istern
Group Chair

DISCUSSION

THE ANANIAS AND SAPPHIRA STORY

The harrowing tale of Ananias and Sapphira is found in Acts: 5:1-11. Some readers of this story may be left wondering what the couple did so wrong and why they had to die? It was the start of the modern church, and people were voluntarily pooling resources and giving to the poor. Ananias and Sapphira, a married couple, chose to sell their land (Acts 5:3), and once it was sold, the money they received remained theirs to do with as they wished (Acts 5:4). When Ananias placed the money at the apostles' feet (Acts 5:2), he donated less than the sale price, but this wasn't the real issue. They could have kept all the money for themselves, kept some and given some away, or offered it all. They also never had to sell their land in the first place if they didn't want to.

However, Ananias made the claim (repeated later by his wife) that the amount of money being given was the same as the sale price of the property. In reality, they had secretly kept some money for themselves but made it appear they had given away every dollar they had received for the sale. By making this false claim, they were lying not just to the apostles but to God (Acts 5:4). God subsequently revealed to Peter what the couple had done, and Peter exposed them.

> Then Peter said, "Ananias, how is it that Satan has so filled your heart that you have lied to the Holy Spirit and have kept for yourself some of the money you received for the land? Didn't it belong to you before it was sold? And after it was sold, wasn't the money at your disposal? What made you think of doing such a thing? You have not lied just to human beings but to God."
>
> *Acts 5:3-4*

At that moment, God's judgement fell upon Ananias, then later upon Sapphira. Their deaths would have served as a strong warning to those present in the meeting.

THE PERSON OF THE HOLY SPIRIT

Peter told Ananias he had lied to the Holy Spirit, in other words, to God. Instead of viewing the Holy Spirit as an individual member of the triune Godhead—three 'persons', one God: Father, Son, and Holy Spirit—some see the Holy Spirit as God's power or divine force. However, you can't lie to an inanimate, non-living power source. You wouldn't say, "I told a lie" to electricity or gravity, or to the wind. This verse shows us the Holy Spirit is a personal being who can be lied to. Similarly, Paul refers to the Holy Spirit as having spoken:

> *Paul had made this final statement: "The Holy Spirit spoke the truth to your forefathers when he said through Isaiah the prophet . . ."*
>
> *Acts 28:25*

Paul also refers to having fellowship with the Holy Spirit:

> *May the grace of the Lord Jesus Christ, and the love of God, and the fellowship of the Holy Spirit be with you all.*
>
> *2 Corinthians 13:14*

We further see how the Holy Spirit expressed his intentions when the church in Antioch was sending out a letter to gentiles regarding observance of the Law:

> It seemed good *to the Holy Spirit and to us not to burden you with anything beyond . . .*
>
> *Acts 15:28*

The Holy Spirit is also recorded as speaking directly to an individual.

> *While Peter was still thinking about the vision, the Spirit said to him, "Simon, three men are looking for you*
>
> *Acts 10:19*

Finally, when it came to water baptism, people were instructed to baptise a person "in the name of the Father and of the Son and of *the Holy Spirit*" (Matthew 28:19).

Why baptise someone into a 'divine force'? It would be like saying, "in the name of the Father, the Son . . . and electricity." We can, therefore, conclude that it makes sense for us to believe that the Holy Spirit is a divine Being and an active member of the Trinity.

LIAR, LIAR, PANTS ON FIRE

Even though they shouldn't, Christians do tell lies on occasion. So, why did Ananias and Sapphira die for that particular sin whereas, today, people don't? Peter tells us that they weren't lying to men (as is most often the case), but rather they were lying directly to God—a far more serious matter. The couple's commitment was divided. They attempted to appear 'saintly' in the eyes of others by making it seem they had given their all. Yet, covetousness and greed had entered their hearts, and they secretly retained some of the funds. We can't serve two masters—God and money (Matthew 6:24). It was important to God that the church started off on the right foot, and the actions of Ananias and Sapphira threatened that. Lying is one of those things that will have no use in heaven; it's best we give it up now.

THE MAN THEY COULDN'T KILL

Arron Ben-Micha
A Chief Priest
Jerusalem Temple

Assassins and Shadow Walkers
Order of the Sicarii Sword
Memphis
Egypt

Date: A.D. 60

(MUST BE DESTROYED AFTER READING)

Dear Sirs,

We have a problem. The problem's name is Paul—although you may remember him as Saul—and we need him dead. He has been promoting false teachings about Jesus which are turning many observant Jews into *unobservant* Jews. Left unchecked, his actions threaten the very future of our religion. Embarrassingly, he was once one of us, having been trained by the great Gamaliel.[129] What I am suggesting will be a difficult job, one that calls for a true professional—a shadow walker of the first order.

Paul previously worked for the temple's internal security unit, rounding up and imprisoning followers of the Jesus conspiracy. While on the road to Damascus one day,[130] he completely lost touch with reality—too much sun, maybe?—and fell victim

---

129 Gamaliel was an expert in Jewish law (Acts 22:3). See also Acts 5:34-39.
130 Acts 9:1-7

to a powerful delusion. Now he travels around deceiving others with his ludicrous belief that Jesus of Nazareth is the long-awaited Messiah. He claims Jesus is the one talked about in the scroll of Isaiah. Stopping him will be far harder to do than one might imagine—trust me, we have tried.

Once we were informed that Paul had gone rogue, we immediately organised some loyal Jews in Damascus to deal with him. Unfortunately, his followers got wind of the plot and lowered him in a basket out through a window in the city wall, where he made good his escape.[131] When he later returned to Jerusalem, a group of Greek Jews tried to kill him. On that occasion, he was again saved by his friends.

Another opportunity presented itself when Paul and some fellow conspirators arrived in Iconium. However, before our plan could get underway, his group travelled to Lystra, twenty miles away. Our Iconium team joined with Jews from Antioch, and together we travelled to Lystra. Before long, our mob had stoned Paul and dragged his body outside the city. Success—or so I thought. Just as I was raising a drink to celebrate, the news arrived that Paul wasn't dead. It turns out 'left for dead' and 'actually dead' aren't the same thing. Somehow, he got back up, returned to the city, and left town the next day.

After spreading lies far and wide, Paul again returned to Jerusalem. This time, we tricked Jews from Asia into believing Paul had brought Greek gentiles into a Jewish-only area of the temple complex, an offence punishable by death. They dragged Paul outside the temple, and soon the crowd was hard at work beating him to death. However, they didn't beat him fast enough. News of the uproar reached the commander of the city's Roman troops, who subsequently took Paul into protective custody. It's ridiculous: You can't find a Roman soldier when you need one, then too many show up when you don't want one.

If I wasn't so certain Paul's teaching and doctrine are wrong, I'd be tempted to believe God was protecting him, which is impossible, of course. I admit that having so many near misses is unnerving—I lose sleep over it if I dwell on it too much. Still, I ask you, can one man escape death *that* many times? Is something more going on, some bigger picture I'm missing? It's as though the man has a divine mission to complete

---

131 Acts 9:25

and nothing can stop him before it's finished. That's impossible, of course. It is we Jews, here at the temple, who were given the divine mission. This Paul is an imposter, I tell you—a fake, a charlatan, a . . . sorry, I'm letting my emotions get the better of me. Best not mention any of this to the High Priest. There was a bit of a stink when Nicodemus joined the Jesus believers, and I wouldn't want him to mistakenly think I was planning on doing the same.

After the Romans rescued Paul, they foolishly let him speak to the crowd to explain himself, and what did he start with? His Damascus Road story! I have a feeling we're never going to hear the end of that stupid tale until he's dead. Thankfully, I'm not the only one who feels that way. Moments after Paul started speaking, the crowd went into an uproar shouting, "Rid the earth of him! He's not fit to live."[132] I couldn't have said it better myself. The difficult part is actually ridding the earth of him—it's like he's glued to the planet or something. The Romans hauled him off to give him a good flogging, and I was thinking we might get lucky, as floggings have killed others. But wasn't to be. Unexpectedly, Paul played his, 'You can't flog me, I'm a Roman citizen' card and got off.[133]

While defending himself before the Sanhedrin against charges arising from the riot, he insulted the High Priest and called him a whitewashed wall. The High Priest has been called a few things in his time, but that was a new one. Moments later, Paul made a reference about his beliefs as a Pharisee, and the next thing you know it was Pharisee versus Sadducee and another uproar had broken out.

While that was going on, we organised more than forty men to bind themselves with an oath not to eat or drink until they had killed Paul. Over forty assassins and only one Paul—the numbers were definitely on our side, and in my mind, he was as good as dead. Sure enough, the plan was foiled. Paul's nephew found out about it and told the Roman commander. Feel free to kill the obnoxious little blabbermouth if you want, I don't care. The commander organised a detachment of two hundred soldiers, seventy horsemen and two hundred spearmen to escort Paul that very night to Caesarea. Suddenly, our

---

132 Acts 22:22
133 Acts 22:25

forty men were up against four hundred and seventy heavily armed Roman troops. The numbers were no longer on our side—we were outnumbered eleven to one.

At Caesarea, Paul was handed over to Governor Felix and put under guard in Herod's palace. Paul appealed to have his case heard by Caesar, but Felix dithered about allowing this and left Paul waiting in jail for two years.[134] Felix was subsequently replaced by Porcius Festus, who we asked to have Paul sent from Caesarea to Jerusalem. We had a plan to ambush Paul on the way and kill him, but Festus wouldn't play ball.[135] Instead, he decided to send Paul to Rome to face Caesar. On his journey to Rome, Paul was shipwrecked (on this occasion we weren't involved), but instead of doing the decent thing and drowning, Paul made it to an island.

As luck would have it, Paul was warming himself by a fire near the shore when a poisonous snake came out of the pile of sticks and bit him.[136] Logic says he should have dropped dead—the snake and I both expected it. If life was fair, he *would* have dropped dead. But you see, he didn't. It's events like this that mess with my mind. How many times can the man miss death by such a whisker? Surviving a stoning that would have killed anyone else, and just happening to find a convenient island after a shipwreck—it's unbelievable, never mind the snake bite! It's as though he's receiving invisible help, but who or what could possibly have reason to give it to him?

Paul has survived no fewer than three shipwrecks, which doesn't mean he *can't* be drowned, although he obviously floats well. He's been beaten with rods, stoned, flogged, and jailed—and still he lives. I'm sure you understand that before any payment is made, we will require absolute proof of Paul's death—'good as dead' just won't do.

Yours,

Arron Ben-Micha
Serving Priest,
Jerusalem Temple

---

134   Acts 24:27
135   Acts 25:3-4
136   Acts 28:3-5

DISCUSSION

After Jesus, Paul is considered the next most significant figure in the New Testament, and he wrote thirteen of its twenty-seven books. Originally a defender of the Jewish religion (Judaism), we first encounter Paul watching Stephen being stoned to death (Acts 7:54-58).

A ROMAN CITIZEN

Paul gained full Roman citizenship[137] by being born in the Roman Empire (in Tarsus—modern Turkey) probably between A.D. 1-5 (Acts 22:28). Roman citizens were not to be flogged or jailed as punishment unless they were first found guilty by trial, a law that saved Paul from a flogging on at least one occasion (Acts 22:24-29) but failed on another.

> *They beat us publicly without a trial, even though we are Roman citizens, and threw us into prison.*
>
> *Acts 16:37*

PAUL'S BACKGROUND

Paul was brought up in Jerusalem (Acts 22:3) and had a sister and a nephew (Acts 23:16). A tent maker by trade, Paul later supported himself financially this way when living in Corinth (Acts 18:3). He could speak Hebrew (Acts 22:2; some versions say, Aramaic) and Greek (Acts 26:14). He stated that he was a true Jewish Israelite (not a convert to Judaism) from the tribe of Benjamin, and was a Hebrew of Hebrews (Philippians 3:5). This final description is probably a reference to the purity of his bloodline (i.e. that he had no gentile blood) or that he could speak Hebrew—not all Jews could at the time. In the Bible he is initially referred to as Saul (or Saul of Tarsus) but after Acts 13:9—only as Paul.[138]

RELIGIOUS TRAINING

> *"My brothers, I am a Pharisee, descended from Pharisees."*
>
> *Acts 23:6*

> *"I was advancing in Judaism beyond many of my own age among my people."*
>
> *Galatians 1:14*

> *"I studied under Gamaliel and was thoroughly trained in the law of our ancestors."*
>
> *Acts 22:3*

The Pharisees were one of several religious sects within Judaism, but one of their key failings was elevating their traditions above the law, a flaw kindly pointed out to them by Jesus.

---

137 There were several different levels of Roman citizenship.

138 Dual names were common (e.g. Matthew was also called Levi). Saul may have always had the name Paul, and changed over to using it, while others think he chose the name Paul after his conversion.

> *And he continued, "You have a fine way of setting aside the commands of God in order to observe your own traditions!*
>
> *Mark 7:9*

Paul was very keen on such traditions, however.

> *[I] was extremely zealous for the traditions of my fathers.*
>
> *Galatians 1:14*

While out in public and with a crowd present, Jesus launched into a detailed seven-point scathing attack on the behaviour and practices of the Pharisees, including this great insult:

> *"You snakes! You brood of vipers!"*
>
> *Matthew 23:33*

JUST THE MAN FOR THE JOB

Paul had the ideal background, training, physical toughness and zeal to take on the task of ushering in a dramatic religious change. As a Pharisee, Paul already believed in the resurrection of the dead, angels, demons, heaven and hell—beliefs common to Christianity. One problem remained: Paul was fully committed to destroying the growing church.

THE ROAD TO DAMASCUS

Having persecuted Christians in Jerusalem, Paul began targetting Christians in Damascus. He headed there carrying letters from the High Priest giving him permission to round up and imprison those belonging to the Way[139] (Acts 9:2). However . . .

> *As he neared Damascus on his journey, suddenly a light from heaven flashed around him. He fell to the ground and heard a voice say to him, "Saul, Saul, why do you persecute me?"*
> *"Who are you, Lord?" Saul asked.*
> *"I am Jesus, whom you are persecuting," he replied.*
> *Saul got up from the ground, but when he opened his eyes he could see nothing. So they led him by the hand into Damascus.*
>
> *Acts 9:3-5, 8*

Paul, the persecutor of Christians had just encountered the resurrected Jesus, changing his life forever. He had been physically blinded by the light but symbolically, he had long been blind to the reality of Jesus. Even today, people still speak of having a 'Damascus Road' experience.

---

139 'The Way' was an early name for Christianity.

ARABIA AND DIVINE REVELATIONS

After his encounter, Paul went travelling:

> . . . I went into Arabia. Later I returned to Damascus. Then after three years, I went up to Jerusalem to get acquainted with Cephas [Peter] and stayed with him fifteen days.
>
> Galatians 1:17-18

During those three years in Arabia,[140] it appears likely that Paul was getting an upgrade to his theology directly from Jesus (and maybe ditching a few of those old Pharisee traditions).

> . . . the gospel I preached is not of human origin. I did not receive it from any man, nor was I taught it; rather, I received it by revelation from Jesus Christ.
>
> Galatians 1:11-12

An unusual event in Paul's life was being taken up into heaven and receiving special revelations (2 Corinthians 12:1-9). To keep him humble after this experience, he was given a 'thorn in his side' (v.7). Some have suggested this 'thorn' was an eyesight issue (Galatians 4:15) while others believe it refers to a person, such as the coppersmith Alexander, who Paul said did him "a great deal of harm" (2 Timothy 4:14). Without more details, Paul's thorn remains unidentifiable.

Paul would spend the rest of his life building and defending the very same church he had previously tried so hard to destroy (Galatians 1:13).

TRAITOR

It must have come as a nasty shock for many at the temple to discover Paul had not only become a believer in Jesus but was actively preaching about him to others, especially to other Jews. He had been trained by their best but had defected to working 'for the other side', making Paul, in their view, a man who had to die.

ASSASSINATION ATTEMPTS

The following attempts on Paul's life take place over a number of years and in various locations:

First: Acts 9:23-25
Second: Acts 9:29-30
Third: Acts 14:4-6
Fourth: Acts 14:19-20
Fifth: Acts 21:30-32
Sixth: Acts 23:12-23
Seventh: Acts 25:3-4 (planned but not executed)

PAUL IN HIS OWN WORDS

Paul's retelling of his Damascus Road experience is recorded in Acts 26:12-16. Paul

---

140 The Arabia mentioned here included land not part of modern Arabia.

gives further biographical details of his life in the following scriptures:

- 2 Corinthians 11:22-28
- Acts 22:3
- Philippians 3:4-6

BODYGUARDS FOR HIRE

Swords of Steel

Close Protection Specialists

Joppa

Paul of Tarsus

C/– Church of Antioch

Antioch City

Date: A.D. 48

Dear Paul,

Roses are red, violets are blue, there's a lot of danger quite close to you. Fear not, however, Swords of Steel are here to provide you with first-class personal protection, with discretion and confidentially assured. Your business remains your business; our business is keeping you alive. I am curious though. You preach, write, and pray for people, yet some of those very people want to flog, stone and otherwise kill you because of it. That strikes me as an extreme response on their part. I've been told you once worked for the temple, detaining and imprisoning those involved with the new Jesus group. Then, after your 'Damascus Road Experience' you gave it all up. I once had a 'Dead Sea Experience' but the only thing that happened was that the weather turned bad, and I got seasick.

I'm sure you don't deliberately seek out dangerous situations—who would? All the same, danger does seem to have an uncanny way of finding you. A shipwreck could happen to anyone (it happened to an aunt of mine once), perhaps even two shipwrecks (my neighbour's cousin suffered the unfortunate experience), but three shipwrecks is unusual. If your dance with danger ended with shipwrecks, I wouldn't bother writing, but your list of mishaps only begins with nautical things and gets progressively worse. Of course, there's also that day and night you spent floating in the ocean without drowning[141]—clever you, it looks like all those after-school swimming lessons your mother bought finally paid off.

In addition to facing water-related dangers, we must also mention the fact you were stoned and left for dead, beaten with rods no fewer than three times, and received forty lashes minus one no less than five times. You were also attacked by angry crowds, thrown into prison, and encountered bandits. I hardly know what to say, other than that I truly fear for your personal safety and consider it a true miracle you're still with us. I'll admit that you've been lucky so far, but luck doesn't provide the same level of certainty a team of Swords of Steel bodyguards can. Whatever enemies you've made previously, they pale in comparison to the ones you've made of late, so please allow us to protect you.

Our protection officers are the best in the business, second to none. They comprise ex-Roman centurions, ex-gladiators (who have won their freedom),[142] and ex-palace guards. They're the best of the best, the toughest of the tough, and the deadliest of the . . . never mind. The important thing is, you'll be well protected twenty-four hours a day. Each man carries a sword as well as two hidden daggers, is an expert with both javelin and spear, and is able to knock a man down at fifty paces using a slingshot. Most can speak several languages.

Each officer is also a master of hand-to-hand combat. The old "I'm a Roman Citizen" line only stops you from being whipped by the Romans; it won't protect you from crazed crowds of fellow Jews or irate sellers of Diana statues.[143] If you stay alive and out of jail, you'll be able to finish writing those letters[144] you're working on, then perhaps you could move on to writing something really interesting. You could even write your autobiography.

---

141 2 Corinthians 11:25

142 Although rare, a gladiator could win their freedom.

143 Acts 19:23-41 Many of the gods had both Greek and Roman names. Romans called this one Diana, while Greeks used the name Artemis.

144 Paul is credited as the author of thirteen of the New Testament letters.

There is no shortage of titles you could use, although suggestions include:

- *Destiny on Damascus Road*
- *The Emmaus Road I Never Travelled*
- *The Pharisee Has Landed*
- *The Curious Incident of Paul in the Light Time*
- *A Tale of Two Pauls*

Anyway, back to my reason for writing. You need professional protection, Paul, and we can provide it for you. Do please come and see me while you're still alive and can discuss your future safety.

Yours,

Marcus Gerwitz
Business Development Manager

DISCUSSION

IMITATE ME AS I IMITATE CHRIST

Paul's life was a mixture of extreme highs and lows. There were the miracles, the healings, the extensive travel he undertook, and the friends he made. He also lost friends, was slandered and rejected by many of his fellow Jews and deserted by some of those he trusted,[145] spent years in prison, and was stoned, beaten, and whipped. His physical body would have carried numerous scars. An extensive list of hardships Paul faced during his life can be found in 2 Corinthians 11:23-27—all of which could have easily been avoided if he simply chose not to preach about Jesus.

For the last two thousand years, hundreds of millions of people have followed in Paul's footsteps and suffered to one degree or another for the sake of the gospel. They have faced emotional or physical hardship,[146] given up riches, titles, fame, recognition and careers, suffered abuse, sacrificed their health and wellbeing, been rejected, and in some cases, even lost their lives. They, too, could have easily avoided such things and had an easier life simply by not preaching Jesus. Why have so many willingly suffered so much for a message that is, according to critics, clearly false?

All who have committed to the gospel message have discovered something within it or had an experience as a result of hearing it that validates it for them. Usually that comes in the form of entering into a personal relationship with Jesus. Subsequently, they are prepared to make different levels of personal sacrifice so that others may hear the message also.

CAESAR WHO?

During his trial in Caesarea, Paul appealed, as was his right as a Roman citizen, to have his case heard by Caesar (Acts 25:11-12). The name Caesar was initially linked to Julius Caesar—a Roman general turned politician who declared himself dictator of the Roman Empire. He had a good start but a bad finish—he was assassinated by rivals just one year later in 44 B.C. Over time, the term Caesar was adopted and used as a title for the Roman Emperor. So, when Paul appealed to 'Caesar', he was appealing to have his case heard by the current 'Caesar' who happened to be Nero (or to his friends, Nero Claudius Caesar Augustus Germanicus—fifth Roman Emperor).

It was Caesar Augustus who issued a decree for the census Joseph and Mary had to undertake (Luke 2:1). Tiberius Caesar is mentioned in Luke 3:1, and finally, there's Caesar Cardini—an Italian who is said to have invented the Caesar salad in the 1920s (he's not in the Bible).

---

145 2 Timothy 2:16, 4:14

146 Adoniram Judson (1788-1850), missionary to Burma (now Myanmar) is one such example.

PASSING THE TORCH

Paul undertook three known missionary trips, and there's speculation as to whether he took a fourth to Spain, having indicated that he wanted to travel there (Romans 15:24). The Book of Acts ends with Paul's future uncertain. Some non-biblical sources suggest he was released from jail, spent time ministering, and was jailed again before being executed. It is likely that he died around A.D. 64 or 65 during a time of persecution against Christians stirred up by Emperor Nero. Even if he had lived longer, the day would have eventually come when he and the original twelve disciples would all be dead. Fortunately, in every generation since, there have been those who have been willing to keep spreading the gospel message despite the hardships involved. Are you up for the challenge?

AND THEN THERE WERE FOUR . . . GOSPELS

Jordan River Publishing Group

Deborah & Barak Towers

Capernaum

The Apostle John

Titus Street

Ephesus

Date: A.D. 68

Dear John,

Thank you for submitting your manuscript *Gospel of John* for possible publication. Synoptic Press has already published the Gospels of Matthew, Mark, and Luke—all of them quite similar in nature. Yours, however, includes plenty of original material. Still, one must ask, is there a need for a fourth Gospel? And if there's a fourth, will there be a fifth or even a sixth? Where does it stop?

In our view, there are several areas that need attention before we can proceed to the next step. First, there is a problem with the 'water into wine' story, as readers are required to do their own calculations to find out the total quantity produced. You mention there were six jars holding an average of twenty-five gallons each, but as schools aren't teaching the twenty-five times table anymore, readers are going to struggle with this. Perhaps, more importantly, was the wine red or white? Details, John, it's all about details. Tell the reader how much wine was made, say whose wedding it was, and describe what the bride was wearing. You've got to remember to cater to your female audience, who are perhaps more into wedding dresses than gallons of wine.

I see you have also provided title suggestions to go with some of the stories, including:

Jesus Washed My Feet

I Was At The Feeding of The Five Thousand

You Could Smell the Perfume in The Room

The Money Changers and The Man with The Whip

Doubt Never Dies—The Thomas Story

A Samaritan Woman Chats About Husbands

Jesus Cooked Me Fish for Breakfast

Peter's Sword and The Missing Ear

I like the story about Nicodemus—the Pharisee who was a member of the Sanhedrin—having a secret night-time meeting with Jesus to discuss religious matters. However, your heading for that section doesn't really capture the air of mystery and intrigue the story invokes. I suggest one of the following instead:

The Night of The Pharisee

To Be Born Again or Not Born Again, That Was His Question

The Man from T.E.M.P.L.E.

Nicodemus—Salvation Revisited

The Pharisee Who Came in from the Shadows

Overall, what you've written is good, but we have a few recommendations:

1. It could do with a bit of spicing up. To help with that, we have enclosed our latest resource: A Writer's Guide to C.O.V.I.D. (Character, Originality, Violence, Intrigue, and Danger). With more COVID in your stories, you'll have thousands if not millions staying home doing nothing but reading, possibly for weeks or even months on end.[147]

---

147 During the global Covid-19 pandemic of 2020-2022, many countries went into periods of 'lockdown', with businesses closed and people staying at, or working from, home.

2. I'm told Jesus ministered for around three-and-a-half years (or one hundred and eighty weeks). Matthew, Mark and Luke all zeroed in on one single week of Jesus's life—his last. Each of them has dedicated almost a third of their Gospel to the events of that week, but I notice you have allocated even more. I understand it was a significant week, but am I missing something? I recommend writing more about some of the other weeks, just to balance things out.

3. In the background notes you supplied, there is mention of someone called Holy Spirit who 'inspired the whole thing'[148] but doesn't want his name on the cover next to yours. I was under the impression this Gospel was entirely your own work, so this will need to be clarified before publication.

4. Should we end up publishing your Gospel, I was thinking of doing a limited run using parchment or vellum.[149] Once printed, you would sign your name inside the cover and we'll promote it as a 'Limited first edition signed by the author', charging extra, of course.

5. If you were to add some extra notes aimed at women—how they were the first to find Jesus's empty tomb and so on, we could create an edition titled, 'The Women's Edition of John's Gospel'. There are others we could do too: Men's Edition, Large Print Edition, Just Out of Jail Edition. The marketing potential is endless, not forgetting a Recovery Edition for anyone who survived a Roman flogging.

6. There is another option worth exploring, although we'd need to first reach an agreement with Matthew, Mark, Peter, Paul, and James. We'd also need to consult with Luke regarding both his Gospel and his latest manuscript, the *Book of Acts*—we're publishing it soon, and it's full of beatings, shipwrecks, angry crowds, lashings, and jailbreaks. Exciting stuff! We even managed to outbid Synoptic Press for the publication rights. Anyhow, the plan would be to assemble all these religious writings into a single publication. Given they all deal with themes such as salvation, personal development and the afterlife, the following title might work well:

---

148 2 Timothy 3:16

149 Vellum was a higher grade of animal skin than parchment, lasting far longer than papyrus paper derived from plants.

B.I.B.L.E. (Believer's Instructions Before Leaving Earth).

Or, to make it sound more intriguing, we could call it:

S.A.F.E. B.I.B.L.E. (Salvation Advice for Everyone, Be Informed Before Life Ends).

Think it over, John, and get back to me when you've decided what to do.

Yours,

Felix Amos
Senior Publishing Consultant

DISCUSSION

present in previously agreed-upon material. A Canon can be *open* and therefore able to receive new entries, or *closed*, meaning no new material can be added.

THE LITERARY CANON

The *Literary Canon* is a collection of writings from ancient to modern that are more than great works—they are viewed as 'essential'. Kaelyn Barron describes the Literary Canon as "an exclusive list where the best classics go to be celebrated and revered for eternity. Admission to the Canon is basically like being granted sainthood for books."[150]

The term 'Canon' comes from the Greek *kanon*, meaning a measuring rod or a standard. When we say that an item has been included as part of a particular Canon, we are saying it measures up to some required standard, which may involve it being compared with other items already part of that Canon. The German composer Ludwig van Beethoven (1770–1827) composed over sixty pieces of music, despite having a degree of hearing loss. His 'Canon of Symphonies', however, is made up of only nine specific pieces.

Exclusion from an official Canon may come about because a work wasn't written by the original author, was produced in a different form, or doesn't hold true to certain ideas or themes

THE CANON OF SCRIPTURE

The full Canon of Scripture[151] (or, the Bible) is in turn, made up of two Canons—the Old and New Testaments. Each of these smaller Canons are an exclusive collection of scrolls, letters or gospels drawn from a larger body of ancient religious writings, each piece having been judged worthy of its inclusion. The Canon of the Old Testament was settled and closed sometime between 400 B.C. and 200 B.C. The exact date depends on who you ask and what exactly one means by 'settled'. The Jewish Bible, or Tanakh[152] contains only 22 books. That said, it has the same content (thus is effectively the same) as the Canon we call the Old Testament, which has 39 books. The reason for the difference is that the later version of the Old Testament Canon separates some of the original books of the Tanakh into several parts, e.g. The Book of Kings became 1st and 2nd Kings in our modern Old Testament.

Around A.D. 370–400, agreement was reached between church leaders regarding the importance of twenty-seven specific pieces of

---

150 www.tckpublishing.com/the-literary-canon/

151 Not to be confused with Canon Law, the legal system of rules used by Catholic, Orthodox and Anglican churches to administer their operations.

152 There is also the term 'Torah', the Jewish name for the first five books of the Old Testament (Genesis, Exodus, Leviticus, Numbers, and Deuteronomy).

writing. Deemed authoritative, they make up the Canon of the New Testament.[153] At this point, the New Testament Canon was considered closed, and no new writings have since been added.

DIVINE INSPIRATION IN THE NEW TESTAMENT

Determining the value of a particular work (especially in the case of New Testament material) included assessing the author and the soundness and accuracy of its teaching and doctrines. It also needed to have wide acceptance amongst existing churches and their leaders. Of particular importance was that a work showed evidence of having been divinely inspired by the Holy Spirit (1 Corinthians 2:13, 2 Peter 1:20-21); in other words, if it wasn't considered 'God-breathed', then it wasn't considered Scripture and was not included in the Bible.

> All Scripture is God-breathed and is useful for teaching, rebuking, correcting and training in righteousness.
>
> *2 Timothy 3:16*

DIVINE INSPIRATION IN THE OLD TESTAMENT

We can see an example of 'God-breathed' writing or 'divine inspiration' at work in the Old Testament where God's thoughts flowed into a person, who then produced them in written form. [The same process the writers of scriptures in the New Testament used]. In 1 Chronicles 28:11-28, where King David gives his son Solomon detailed written instructions and plans for the building of the first temple, we read:

> He gave him the plans of all that the Spirit had put in his mind for the courts of the temple of the Lord.
>
> *v.12*

King David received the building plans from God via the Holy Spirit (the divine inspiration part) then wrote them down so he could pass them on to his son Solomon.

> "All this," [the plans] David said, "I have in writing as a result of the LORD's hand on me, and he enabled me to understand all the details of the plan."
>
> *v.19*

Not only did King David receive the information from God, he was also enabled to understand the details. Inspiration is not limited to data alone; it can include knowledge and understanding.

New Zealand theologian James MacGregor (1829-1894) observed that we should reject any notion that Scripture was an exercise in

---

153 The Protestant Canon has 66 books; 39 Old Testament, 27 New Testament, together comprising the Bible. The canon of the Catholic and Orthodox churches include additional Old Testament books which the Protestant church doesn't recognise. That said, all three branches of the church (Protestant, Catholic and Orthodox) have the same books in their New Testament.

mechanical dictation. Rather, as the Holy Spirit expressed his thoughts, feelings or desires, these were written down by a person using their own words (unless instructed otherwise). Although each work is inspired, each also reflects the unique writing style and word choice of the individual author, making the result a mixture of divine and human effort. As observed by the late Bruce Metzger (previously a professor at Princeton Theological Seminary), we should view the biblical Canon as a list of authoritative books (and they are authoritative because they are God-inspired), rather than an authoritative list of books.

EXCLUSION FROM THE CANON

Other books may have been written by an apostle or even labelled a 'gospel', but this alone wasn't enough to warrant inclusion in the biblical Canon. The Bible itself refers to various works that didn't end up being included amongst its pages. These include the *Book of Jasher* (Joshua 10:13) and *Visions of Iddo the Seer* (2 Chronicles 9:29). Along with

inspiring the writers of Scripture, I believe God would have directed and influenced the process by which writings were selected for inclusion.

People sometimes claim a particular piece of ancient writing (and some are dragged up with monotonous regularity) should have been included in the Bible, especially the New Testament. Many of these works were written long after (i.e. several centuries) the New Testament Canon was closed. In short, they came along far too late for consideration. Furthermore, most of these works would never have been suitable anyway, as they contained teachings and doctrines that were false and/or contradictory compared to existing biblical writings. Furthermore, even those few documents that may have been theologically accurate were still omitted because they lacked the 'divine inspiration' factor. Christianity has established itself, grown and continued from generation to generation using the original (be it ancient) Canon of the Bible. Clearly, its contents, as they are today, are doing the job just fine.

TREATING WOMEN THE WRONG WAY

The Torah Team
Law Observation Division
Sheep Gate Alley

Andrew the Apostle
The Way HQ
Jerusalem

Date: A.D. 34

Dear Andrew,

Firstly, may I say how nice it is to hear that you and the other disciples are continuing the work Jesus started. Your group's approach to religious matters is a most refreshing one, especially compared to how things have been done up until now. Nevertheless, there is one thing Jesus did which you are repeating, and it needs to stop. You are giving women too much prominence—elevating their status to levels in excess of what they deserve. I can overlook Jesus helping out his mother with some extra wine at a wedding, but it should have ended there. He definitely shouldn't have gone on to treat other women the way he did.

Take that woman who was brought to him after being caught in adultery,[154] for example. She should have been stoned—it was an open and shut case really—yet he allowed her to live. Then there was the time Jesus talked to that Samaritan woman.[155] She was at

---

154 John 8:3-11
155 John 4:4-42

the well in the middle of the day *by herself*. Given that the other women didn't want to associate with her, she was clearly an outcast, even amongst her own people. Worse still, she had rushed through husbands faster than people scramble to get into the disturbed waters at the pool of Bethsaida.[156] If Jesus felt he had to talk to a Samaritan—and goodness knows why anyone would—could he not at least have made it a man?

On another occasion, Jesus received an urgent plea from an important synagogue leader named Jairus. His twelve-year-old child was sick and dying,[157] and Jesus was on his way to help. But lurking in the crowd was a woman—not just any woman, but one who was unclean due to ongoing bleeding. She'd had the blood thing for twelve years[158] so she could easily have waited a little longer, but she didn't—so selfish of her. There's no way a ceremonially unclean woman like her should have been out in public in the first place, risking making others unclean. I'm sure you know the rules from the scroll of Numbers[159]—unclean touches clean, clean becomes unclean.

This self-entitled woman pushed through the crowd and deceitfully snuck up behind[160] Jesus, so he couldn't see her coming. Once close enough, she reached out and touched the hem of the garment he was wearing. The audacity of the woman to do that when, somewhere, a little child lay dying, the father desperate. Jesus stopped and healed the woman, which was definitely the wrong thing for him to have done. What was he thinking? Things worked out fine for the woman but then news arrived that Jairus's child had died.[161] That's not fine, is it? Not only did a child die, but because the woman touched Jesus's garment, *he* was made unclean.[162] All this hassle because one selfish, interfering woman couldn't wait her turn in line. I'd be happy to tell you more, but I didn't hear what happened next.

---

156 John 5:2-9
157 Luke 8:41-42
158 Luke 8:43-48
159 Numbers 19:22
160 Mark 5:27
161 Luke 8:49
162 Leviticus 15:27

On another occasion, Jesus was in a synagogue teaching on the Sabbath. There was a woman sitting at the back, keeping quiet like she should. Then, Jesus surprised everyone by inviting her to come to the front. The woman was bent over; she had been that way for eighteen years.[163] The sight of her condition alone would have been enough to put people off their lunch. Those attending hadn't come to have their time wasted. Yet, Jesus made everyone wait for some deformed old woman to slowly shuffle the length of the synagogue, and when she finally got to the front, he healed her. Couldn't he have done that at her house, in private? Why do it in public? Why treat her with such dignity? Why give preferential treatment to her when there were men present?

Finally, there's that Mary Magdalene woman—a true sinner if ever there was one. How many devils were cast out of her? One, two? No, wait, I remember—it was seven![164] It's hard to imagine there was enough room to fit them all in. Now this is a woman who's lived a life more scarlet than the curtains in Rahab's bordello and has a blacker past than the accumulated sins of King Ahab. Yet Jesus not only associated with her but gave her one of the most significant tasks in all of history—the honour of telling the disciples that he'd risen from the dead.[165] If there was ever a job for a man, this was it, yet Jesus gave it to a *woman*. The only explanation I can think of to explain his choice is that his returning to life even further clouded his judgement concerning women.

Do you and the other disciples intend to carry on this stupidity of treating women so respectfully? If so, you can count me out! I'll be sticking with that other lot at the temple. When it comes to women, they at least know how to keep them in their place.

Yours,

Omer

---

163 Luke 13:10–11

164 Luke 8:2

165 Matthew 28:1-10

DISCUSSION

WOMEN: WORTHY OF VALUE

Of the many contributions Christianity has made to history, its elevation of the status of women is one of the most significant. The longest continuous conversation recorded in the New Testament is between Jesus and a woman—the woman he met at the well (see John chapter four). Jesus's treatment of women—which went against many of the cultural norms of the day—became a model for his disciples and for the church. With regard to women, Jesus:

- Treated them with respect
- Allowed them to travel with him as part of his team
- Crossed cultural and social boundaries to interact with them
- Indicated it was important for them to learn spiritual teachings (Luke 10:42)
- Ate with them
- Offered salvation on equal terms as men
- Honoured them in public situations
- Relied on their financial assistance (Luke 8:2-3)
- Had some as personal friends (Mary and Martha—sisters of Lazarus)

FAITH ALONE SAVES

Some have tried to claim that Christianity, or Paul specifically, is anti-women. In Acts 16:12, Paul and his travelling companions arrived in Philippi, a Roman colony. The following day, they met a group of women praying by the river. One was Lydia, a seller of purple cloth and described as a 'worshipper of God'. Lydia listened to Paul's message and came to believe in Jesus. Even for those who already believed in God, as she did, Paul preached that a further step was now required—to repent and put their faith in Jesus for salvation.

> I have declared to both Jews and Greeks that they must turn to God in repentance and have faith in our Lord Jesus.
>
> *Acts 20:21*

There is a big difference between saying, "I believe in God" and "I have put my faith in Jesus Christ as my Lord and Saviour." You can find plenty of politicians who will make the first statement but not many who will declare the second. Lydia believed in God, but upon hearing about Jesus, she had to take a further step—to repent and place her faith in him alone.

WAS PAUL ANTI-WOMEN?

Lydia invited Paul and his companions to come and *stay* at her house. Sometime later, Paul returned there again (Acts 16:40). If he had been so obnoxiously anti-women, it's unlikely he would have been welcomed for a first visit, let alone a second. Paul also lived and worked with Aquila and his wife Priscilla for eighteen months (Acts 18:2-3,11). Even if Paul was anti-women, it doesn't match the example set by Jesus and is thus not a true reflection of God or of Christianity. Furthermore, we consistently read of women interacting with Paul so positively, such as when they gave him a warm welcome when he returned to Jerusalem (Acts 21:17). Paul also speaks warmly of nine different women in Romans 16.

Yes, yes, but didn't Paul say women had to stay silent? That proves he was anti-women, doesn't it? Well, it's true Paul wrote:

> Women should remain silent in the churches. They are not allowed to speak, but must be in submission, as the law says.
>
> 1 Corinthians 14:34

Does this mean women cannot pray or sing in church? Does it mean a woman can't witness to a non-believer about Jesus while in church? The Bible encourages us *all* to pray without ceasing (1 Thessalonians 5:17). Paul also wrote: "But if an inquirer or unbeliever comes in while *everyone* is prophesying" (1 Corinthians 14:24) and "When you come together, *each of you* has a hymn, or a word of instruction . . ." (1 Corinthians 14:26).

So, women must stay silent, but women can also prophesy and sing hymns? As you can't sing a hymn while remaining silent, we need to recognise there are issues of context involved with these particular writings about women. It's likely that Paul's instructions in 1 Corinthians 14:13 were intended to target a very specific situation, outside of the common practices of singing and praying regularly occurring in a church meeting.

JAIRUS'S DAUGHTER

Was Jesus made unclean when his clothes were touched by the unclean woman in Luke 8? Interpretations on this differ. Some say that his clothing, not his physical body, was touched. Regardless, when he arrived at Jairus's house he continued to minister (Luke 8:54), something he should not have done if he was in an unclean state. And what happened to the young child who died? Jesus arrived at Jairus's house and raised the young girl back to life.

LIFE LIVED TO THE FULL

People have complained about Christianity's historical treatment of women, but when stacked up against other religions, it has nothing to be ashamed of. It is important that any modern analysis of Christianity's stance on women be based on New Testament writings *and not* on the actions and claims of a few who implement it incorrectly. Despite the misguided claims of some men, the New Testament does not say that a wife has to submit to *everything* her husband wants. In contrast to some religions, Christianity does not require a husband or wife to accept physical, sexual, or verbal abuse and violence within a marriage. Neither does the Bible say that a woman:

- Has to stay at home and not go to work
- Must only wear dresses and not trousers
- Must be accompanied by her husband or male relative when going out
- Must grow her hair long, or wear a scarf, or fully cover her body
- May not undertake higher levels of education

Christianity doesn't say women are valuable because they can bear children, look good in certain clothing, or because they can work like men. The Bible says a woman is valuable in her own right because, as a human, she was made in and carries the *Imago Dei* [latin], that is, the Image of God. All women are created in the image of God (Genesis 1:27), therefore, all women have value.

In John 10:10, Jesus said, that the reason he came, was so "... they may have life, and have it to the full" (or according to some translations: "have it abundantly"). That statement applies equally for both men and women.

PRISON PROBLEMS

Office of the Inspector General of Jails
Department of Jurisprudence & Courts
Jerusalem

Chains, Shackles, and Leg Irons Ltd
Ocean Promenade
Caesarea Maritima

Date: A.D. 51

Re: Equipment failure and escape of prisoners

Dear Justus,

I have just finished reading a very unsettling report that identifies multiple occasions where hardware you supplied to our jails has failed, allowing prisoners to escape. Let me explain further. Several of Jesus's disciples, who were making a nuisance of themselves in Solomon's Colonnade[166] were arrested on the High Priest's orders and put in the public jail.[167] The next morning, their cells were open and they had disappeared. Locals were calling it "The Great Escape." Extra guards had to be hired, which threw the annual operating budget out the window.

Things had barely settled down when King Herod Agrippa had Peter arrested and imprisoned. Not wanting to risk another 'great escape', he ordered that sixteen guards—four squads of four soldiers—be used to guard Peter. He was chained directly to two of them, and two further guards acted as sentries at the prison entrance. Secure? You would think so. After all, he was shackled with chains and stocks from *your* company. Yet during the morning rounds, it was discovered that all the guards were present, but

---

166 Solomon's Colonnade (aka Solomon's Porch) was part of the temple complex.

167 Acts 5:17-26

Peter wasn't.[168] Sometime during the night, the chains you supplied failed, and Peter was able to free himself and escape. Herod was not pleased. I was not pleased. Herod was so angry, he had sixteen of my guards executed.[169] Now, I was angry. I had sixteen funerals to attend, and on top of that, I had to make arrangements for sixteen new guards to be employed. Graffiti soon began appearing, hindering our recruitment efforts. Some of it read:

Work for the jail service. Get executed before your prisoner does.

Peter +1 | Guards -16

Game, set, and match to Peter!

With sixteen fewer staff, existing staff had to work double shifts. The number of staff calling in sick skyrocketed. You can imagine the effect all of this was having on the overtime budget . . . as I said, completely out the window.

Thankfully, a few years of normality followed, but several days ago another incident involving your hardware occurred. Paul and his assistant Silas were in Philippi and, after an uproar, found themselves in jail. They were stripped and beaten,[170] and their jailer given specific instructions to guard them carefully. He did this by putting them in the innermost cell and locking their feet in stocks—stocks *you* supplied, stocks that should have made them secure—at least, you would think so, considering how much the jail service paid for them. "Good, solid stocks," the sales brochure said. Paul and Silas certainly didn't look like they were going anywhere, but then again, neither did Peter before he vanished.

Around midnight—when normal people are sleeping—those two nutcases started singing. What sort of weirdos sit naked in jail singing at midnight? Don't answer that. Then, it happened. The chains failed, the door locks failed, and the prison doors swung open.[171] It was not only the door on Paul and Silas's cell but the doors on every cell.

---

168 Acts 12:3-10
169 Acts 12:18-19
170 Acts 16:22-24
171 Acts 16:26

Equipment failures were happening faster than we could count them, leaving the jailer so distraught he was about to kill himself, or so I am told.[172]

It is clear that you've sold us equipment at full price, but not at full quality. Perhaps a week or two inside one of our fine jails clamped inside some of your own leg irons may help you determine the exact nature of the problem. I've received a note from the emperor with a 'please explain' request. I'll make sure to mention your name when I see him.

Frankly, I don't care if a few people die in prison while awaiting their death sentence by whipping or crucifixion—ultimately, they still end up dead. What I do care about is if prisoners escape on my watch. Beginning next week, we will be testing all locks, stocks, chains and leg irons for weaknesses or faults. We will be assisted by Masada Lock & Key Co. Don't go taking any holidays until you have heard from me further.

I will keep you updated.

Yours,

Quintus Maximus Meridius
Commander, Jails of the North

---

172 Acts 16:27

205

DISCUSSION

PRISONERS FOR CHRIST

There are many references in the Bible to God's followers being thrown in jail. Paul even boasted of having a 'frequent user' card.

> *I have worked much harder, been in prison more frequently . . .*
> *2 Corinthians 11:23*

Many, like Joseph in Genesis 39, were imprisoned after being wrongfully accused (Genesis 39:11-20). Unfortunately, wrongful convictions have continued over the centuries, many occurring as a result of corrupt police or judicial systems or poor criminal investigations.

A FISH ON A HOOK

Prisons don't always come with bars; we can find ourselves 'imprisoned' by many things—our own behaviour, circumstances, health, or a financial situation. People sometimes say they are 'imprisoned by debt' or feel like 'a prisoner in my own home'. Sin, too, can imprison a person. The Bible tells us that the pleasures of sin are 'fleeting' (Hebrews 11:25) but ultimately, left undealt with, sin will imprison and enslave us. Think of a hook, baited with a 'pleasurable and desirable' morsel that the fish enjoys for a

moment. But when the hook strikes, the fish finds itself enslaved, with its future at risk.

Peter mentions how some people, already enslaved by sinful behaviour, try enticing others along (2 Peter 2:19). Generally, sinners love company. Sin doesn't feel so bad if you know others are doing it, too. A single protestor might not walk into a no-go zone, but a protesting crowd will. When a majority are doing something, they may even turn on those who aren't joining in, claiming there's something wrong with them, or that they are holding onto outdated behaviours or morals: "You're still following the Bible's rules? You dinosaur!"

SETTING CAPTIVES FREE

Many Christian organisations and churches work with prisons and prisoners. One example of this is Prison Fellowship, started by a man named Chuck (Charles) Colson. For four years, Chuck Colson served in the White House as chief counsel for President Richard Nixon. On a television broadcast in 1973, Nixon said the following:

> "People have got to know whether or not their President's a crook. Well, I'm not a crook."[173]

When a country's President goes on television to tell the nation he isn't a crook, you know something isn't going to end well. Sure enough, both President Nixon and Chuck

---

173 www.history.com/this-day-in-history/nixon-insists-that-he-is-not-a-crook

Colson were tied up with a series of events that became known as 'the Watergate scandal'. Nixon became the first United States president to resign while still in office, and Colson ended up serving prison time. He later became a Christian and started the ministry now known as Prison Fellowship International (PFI). According to their website, PFI operates in over one hundred countries with over fifty thousand volunteers.[174]

ONLY A PRAYER AWAY

There is some speculation as to whether Paul ever spent time in Rome's notorious Mamertine Prison. Viewed by some as the worst of the worst, it was an extremely unpleasant place. Whether your prison comes with bars or not, there is no place—however remote, dark, dank, depressing, or filthy—where God cannot reach you. No matter your location, no matter if your emotional state is positive or if you are in the deepest pit of despair, God is able to reach out and meet you in your moment of need. God's presence is everywhere—high or low, in the darkest dark, or even in some remote prison (Psalm 139). Wherever you are in the world, he is always only a prayer away.

Where can I go from your Spirit? Where can I flee from your presence?

Psalm 139:7

---

174 www.devex.com/organizations/prison-fellowship-international-pfi-48440

THE BIGGEST CHANGE
SINCE SLICED BREAD

Malachi
A Concerned Jew
Jerusalem

The Apostle Paul
Church of Antioch
Antioch City

Date: A.D. 48

Dear Paul,

I understand you've been feeling sorry for the gentiles. Well, that's because you spend far too much time associating with them. As a result, you've developed an unbalanced sense of priorities, and your thinking on religious matters has become distorted. Take, for example, your latest plan promoting a reduction in the number of items of the Law that gentile believers must observe. What are you calling this new approach: Judaism Lite? Just because you tricked the leaders of your group in Jerusalem into agreeing with you on the matter doesn't make it right, you know.

I hear your friend James has gone so far as even to release a directive on the matter.[175] Of the original six hundred and thirteen items of the Law found in the sacred scrolls, you now say that believers only need to obey a *handful*. At least you're telling them they still need to keep the part about not engaging in sexually immoral practices. And you've kept the bit about not engaging with the occult, so at least you haven't completely

---

175 Acts 15:13-20

lost touch with reality. The issue is, you've ditched adherence to almost every food, clothing and ceremonial requirement there ever was. You really mustn't pander to gentiles, letting them ignore most of Deuteronomy and Leviticus just to win favour with them. Moses is likely turning in his grave—or he would be, if we could find it.[176]

Under your new approach, it won't be long until gentile believers begin selling bacon[177] and egg pies a stone's throw from the temple or eating scallops[178] for dinner. Shame on you, Paul—you and your lot are being far too liberal. Whatever you are currently promoting, it certainly isn't what you and I grew up with. All these changes aren't the way to attract gentiles to God. Sell them sackcloth at half price if you must, or halve their temple tax instead.

If these Jesus-believers get away with *not* observing the Law, there will be major implications for the temple—or don't you care anymore? Gentile believers in Jesus, and any Jews who join them (I hear there's been more than a few—traitors, all of them), *won't* have to make an annual visit, or indeed *any* temple visit during their lifetime.[179] Travel companies offering package tours for Passover will suffer and may even go bankrupt.

You teach that Jesus sacrificed himself as the perfect lamb of God to take away the sins of the world, but I ask you, what is wrong with the perfectly good lambs they're using at the temple currently? The long-term implications of your changes are terrifying. If your new approach is valid, and I know you believe it is, there will end up being unemployed animal sellers and probably more than a few Levite priests begging for money on street corners. The whole economy could face collapse.

For thousands of years, we Jews have been set apart as God's chosen people. Now you say God always intended gentiles to be included in his salvation plan? All I can say is, he certainly kept that quiet. I can't see the chief priests buying it—you'd have to destroy the temple to stop them keeping with the current system, and even that might not be

---

176 Deuteronomy 34:5-6

177 Leviticus 11:7

178 Leviticus 11:10 (For more about food rules, see 1 Timothy 4:4-5; Mark 7:15; Colossians 2:16).

179 Deuteronomy 16:16

enough.[180] If that happened—a destroyed temple is unthinkable, of course—the land it's on would become little more than a large piece of very desirable real estate, a tourist attraction at best with people wailing at the walls.[181] I know God won't allow it; that would equate to him giving his approval to your new teachings.

What you are promoting has lit the fuse on something far larger than you, Paul. If this isn't stopped, it'll end up reshaping the entire world, you mark my words. And if you are right, think how crowded the afterlife will be—millions, even billions of extra people. I'm appalled at the very thought of it, Jews and gentiles packed into eternity like sardines all because of your crazy ideas. How dare you ruin eternity for me! It might be a cruel thing to say, but it might be better for everyone if you went off and drowned in a shipwreck, or something of the sort. You must stop this foolishness now—although I'm already beginning to fear it's too late.

Yours,

Malachi

---

180 Some Jews still talk about building a third temple in Jerusalem.

181 Observant Jews still pray at a section of the Temple Mount support wall referred to as the Western Wall or Wailing Wall.

DISCUSSION

MAKING THE SHIFT

From the moment of Jesus's death on the cross, it was clear that things were not going to remain as they were. As Jesus died, the curtain in the temple tore from top to bottom, opening wide the 'Holy of Holies' to all people. It represented a new and living way for people to interact with God directly, rather than requiring the efforts of a priest. This torn curtain can be viewed as the 'tip of the iceberg' concerning a package of changes God had for his followers. For early believers in Jesus, the shift from Judaism, based on the Old Covenant law, to New Covenant Christianity was a bumpy one, involving social, cultural and religious clashes.

God used Peter's rooftop vision in Acts 10:9-27 to start the ball rolling in the area of Jewish-gentile relations. Here, God laid out clear ground rules (Acts 10:15), and gentiles—previously considered 'outsiders' and even 'unclean'—were now, on God's orders, part of the club. God had always intended this, but now that this ancient plan was coming to pass, there were, unsurprisingly, a few teething problems.

Priests acting as mediators between people and God had now been done away with, as had animal sacrifices for sin. Instead, one could now come to God directly for forgiveness. People no longer needed to be declared 'clean' from things such as skin infections—a rather lengthy process according to Leviticus 14:1-20. The New Covenant also included changes that were specific to food. Certain 'old school' Jewish groups put pressure on the new 'Jesus converts' to follow the Law, including eating only 'kosher' food—that is, food permitted under the Old Testament Law. Paul and others, however, weren't convinced that these things were still required. After consulting together in Jerusalem, the apostles and elders sent a letter of guidance back with Paul to his home church in Antioch (Acts 15:1-35). The letter's main message was as follows:

> *It seemed good to the Holy Spirit and to us not to burden you with anything beyond the following requirements: You are to abstain from food sacrificed to idols, from blood, from the meat of strangled animals and from sexual immorality. You will do well to avoid these things.*
>
> *Acts 15:28-29*

While parts of the moral law remained in effect, primarily those covering issues like murder, lying, and stealing, changing from living 'under the law' to living 'under grace' gave Christians enormous freedom in how they lived out their faith. It was this new-found freedom that made some traditional Jews jealous and angry (Galatians 2:4).

TAKING IT GLOBAL

Although it was probably not so obvious at the time, this 'new covenant' also freed Christianity to become a global faith. The requirement to assemble regularly in Jerusalem (Deuteronomy 16:16) for sacrifices or ceremonies was gone. A person no longer needed a priest to mediate between themselves and God, as Jesus now fulfilled that role (1 Timothy 2:5). People could now live anywhere in the world and never set foot in Jerusalem unless they were a tourist. Their location no longer mattered in terms of living out the Christian faith and connecting with God.

There was no requirement about wearing certain fabrics or praying in a certain place. People could pray and read the Scriptures in their own language, and with food options now including almost anything that could be eaten, a person living in any country could follow Christianity without dietary difficulty. Of course, that is not to say one doesn't need to choose wisely what they eat—unhealthy diets, even if made up from permitted food, can still lead to undesirable outcomes.

'JESUS ONLY' SALVATION

Ever since New Testament times, there has been an ongoing battle to keep Christians from being drawn back into following certain aspects of the Old Testament Law—or into making their own traditions into new laws! Even Peter (Cephas) was drawn back to the old ways, taking Barnabas with him. When Paul found out what Peter had done, he gave him a good tongue lashing and sent him to the naughty corner (Galatians 2:11-14).

One still comes across churches that tell women how they must dress, while others try to limit which musical instruments can be played during a church service. There are those who promote keeping Old Testament food rules (no ham sandwiches for the shared lunch, thank you very much) or insist that only a certain version of the Bible—usually the King James Version—is the 'correct one'. Some make paying of tithes compulsory or claim certain practices—such as weekly church attendance or regular witnessing in the community—are required to maintain salvation.

Our salvation is a 'Jesus only' salvation, not a 'Jesus plus' salvation. The 'Jesus plus' brigade would have you believe that in addition to knowing Jesus, you need to do something more, like witnessing or paying tithes, in order to be saved. Legalism tries to bring people back under the Law, but Jesus sets us free from it (Romans 8:2). The Bible gives firm, clear reasons why Christians should refuse to follow the Old Testament law in order to seek right standing before God:

1. You are under a curse if you do (Galatians 3:10)
2. Salvation can't be obtained through observing the law (Galatians 3:11)
3. If you are keeping the Law, you must keep all of it perfectly (James 2:10)
4. Jesus saves us by his grace, not as a result of our ability to keep the law (Ephesians 2:8-9)

Fundamental changes introduced during the first century, along with the teachings written into the New Testament, resulted in Christianity becoming a fully portable, self-contained, go anywhere, fit-any-culture belief system. Most importantly, it is completely voluntary. Jesus invites people into relationship but doesn't force or coerce people. One may leave at any time.

A FLOURISHING, LIVING FAITH

Starting in Jerusalem some two thousand years ago, Christianity has grown to become the belief system with the largest number of followers. It has withstood centuries of opposition and attack, both physical and intellectual, yet remains steadfast and continues attracting new adherents worldwide.

For two thousand years, the Christian faith has provided billions of people with hope, purpose, and a reason for living. When it comes to choosing a living faith, never be tempted to settle for anything less than a genuine, eternal relationship with Jesus Christ—the one who sacrificed his life for you. It's the very best that money *can't* buy, and billions have staked their lives on it. Will you?

STAY CONNECTED

For speaking requests or to get in touch with the author,

please email: 40letters@inspire.net.nz

ACKNOWLEDGEMENTS

Like a good cheese, this book has taken time, and hopefully, as a result, readers will find it tasty to read and spiritually nutritional. Along the way I had help, and so, to my wife, family and friends who provided their honest feedback, timely encouragement, useful suggestions, and made me coffee, I say thank you.

Special thanks to Kirsty Kirk for proofreading many, many letters including some that didn't make the final cut. Secondly, to Doug Stewart for his spiritual support, keeping me on-topic in the discussion sections and for always believing the book would be finished by Christmas, without ever saying which Christmas—there were several.

Turning the manuscript into an actual book was undertaken by Anya and Jeff McKee and their talented team at Torn Curtain Publishing. My thanks to Anya for her professional editing skills along with all the other assistance she provided. Jeff's talents made sure the book's letters looked like real letters and gave the discussion sections a bitesize, easy-to-read layout. Of course, I could have done it all without any of them, but the book would have been a terrible mess, filled with grammatical and historical errors and virtually unreadable.

Lastly, to anyone who purchased the book through a reseller—thank you. You've made my fantasy of owning a $500 million luxury super yacht in which to cruise the Mediterranean in my retirement several dollars closer.

Interested in finding out more about Christianity?

https://alpha.org/